FINANCIAL CRISIS IN AMERICA

FINANCIAL CRISIS IN AMERICA

RAYMUND T. OVANHOUSER
EDITOR

Nova Science Publishers, Inc.
New York

For permission to use material from this book please contact us:
Telephone 631-231-7269; Fax 631-231-8175
Web Site: http://www.novapublishers.com

LIBRARY OF CONGRESS CATALOGING-IN-PUBLICATION DATA

Ovanhouser, Raymond T.

Financial crisis in America / Raymond T. Ovanhouser.

p. cm.

Includes index.

ISBN 978-1-60692-191-3 (hardcover)

1. Financial crises--United States. 2. Subprime mortgage loans--United States. 3. Mortgage loans--United States. 4. Housing--United States--Finance. 5. United States--Economic conditions--21st century. I. Title.

HB3722.O85 2009

330.973--dc22

2008047889

Published by Nova Science Publishers, Inc. ✢ New York

CONTENTS

PREFACE

There is no precise definition of "financial crisis," but a common view is that disruptions in financial markets rise to the level of a crisis when the flow of credit to households and businesses is constrained and the real economy of goods and services is adversely affected. Since mid-2007, central bankers — including the Federal Reserve — have labored to keep the downturn in U.S. subprime housing from developing into such a crisis. While subprime problems were widely anticipated, the subsequent spread of turmoil into many seemingly unrelated parts of the global financial system was not.

Many losses occurring in diverse firms and markets — often quite severe — have features in common: the use of complex, hard-to-value financial instruments; large speculative positions underwritten by borrowed funds, or leverage; and the use of off-the-books entities to remove risky trading activities from the balance sheets of major financial institutions. It is not yet clear whether financial market problems will significantly slow the economy: many believe that the current episode is simply the downside of a normal credit cycle, that is, a natural corrective to several years of unusually easy credit conditions. On the other hand, some analysts identify market dynamics that may amplify the effects of financial shocks and have the potential to generate self-reinforcing, downward financial and economic spirals. The Federal Reserve has used its traditional tools to avert such an outcome: it has lowered short-term interest rates dramatically and injected billions of dollars into the banking system to support market liquidity and keep credit flowing. In addition, the Fed has expanded its sphere by making funds available to securities firms, which it does not regulate, and has provided funding to underwrite the rescue-through-acquisition of Bear Stearns, a leading investment bank.

The duration of the current instability is in marked contrast to financial shocks of recent decades — stock market crashes, bond market disruptions, the

9/11 attacks — when the central bank was able to contain market problems quickly with little or no interruption of U.S. economic growth. Depending on how soon normal market conditions are restored, and at what cost, policy makers may consider whether regulators have access to adequate information about market conditions, and whether currently unregulated market participants should be subjected to disclosure and reporting requirements.

In addition, the social costs of failed financial speculation may be judged great enough to warrant new restrictions designed to lower the incidence of losses that have system-wide impacts or to put the markets and the economy in a better position to weather such shocks.

Chapter 2 - Firms are said to be liquid when they are able to meet current obligations or short-term demand for funds. A firm is said to be solvent but illiquid when its assets exceed its liabilities but it is unable to liquidate assets rapidly enough to meet current obligations. Markets are said to be liquid when a large volume of financial securities can be traded without price distortions because there is a ready and willing supply of buyers and sellers. Liquid markets are a sign of normalcy.

In August 2007, liquidity abruptly dried up for many firms and securities markets. Suddenly some firms were able to borrow and investors were able to sell certain securities only at prohibitive rates and prices, if at all. The liquidity crunch was most extreme for firms and securities with links to subprime mortgages, but it also spread rapidly into seemingly unrelated areas. The stock market experienced unusual volatility and investors rushed to buy the safest of all investments, U.S. Treasury securities. On August 31, Federal Reserve Chairman Ben Bernanke noted that "[a]lthough this episode appears to have been triggered largely by heightened concerns about subprime mortgages, global financial losses have far exceeded even the most pessimistic projections of credit losses on those loans."

The spread of disruptions from housing into other debt markets is an example of financial contagion, or systemic risk. Contagion spread among non-bank institutions: mortgage lenders, hedge funds, and issuers of various types of securities, including commercial paper, asset-backed securities, structured products, and debt supporting leveraged buyouts and takeovers. As fear of risk has increased, these institutions saw sources of credit vanish and struggled to meet existing financing commitments, to post additional collateral, and to cope with portfolio losses. Some financial institutions, primarily mortgage lenders and hedge funds, have been unable to resolve liquidity problems and have closed. In the months ahead, there may be more failures.

Central banks, including the Federal Reserve, have responded by providing liquidity — injecting cash into the banking system and lowering interest rates —

in order to prevent financial disruptions from slowing real economic growth. While financial "paper losses" have no direct effect on output or employment, there are channels through which changes in financial conditions may be transmitted to the real economy: for example, tight credit and equity markets restrain business investment in plant and equipment.

In the wake of the liquidity crunch, policymakers may consider several areas for reform. Could regulation have prevented current problems in the mortgage market? Should credit rating agencies, like Moody's and Standard and Poor's, be subject to more oversight by the Securities and Exchange Commission? Should the non-bank institutions that have been central to this episode be subject to greater regulatory supervision or information disclosure requirements? This chapter analyzes the causes, progress, and broad policy issues raised by recent liquidity problems, but does not address proposals to alleviate distress in the housing sector.

Chapter 3 - There is no precise definition of "financial crisis," but a common view is that disruptions in financial markets rise to the level of a crisis when the flow of credit to households and businesses is constrained and the real economy of goods and services is adversely affected. Since mid-2007, central bankers — including the Federal Reserve — have labored to keep the downturn in U.S. subprime housing from developing into such a crisis.

While subprime problems were widely anticipated, the subsequent spread of turmoil into many seemingly unrelated parts of the global financial system was not. Many losses occurring in diverse firms and markets — often quite severe — have features in common: the use of complex, hard-to-value financial instruments; large speculative positions underwritten by borrowed funds, or leverage; and the use of off-the-books entities to remove risky trading activities from the balance sheets of major financial institutions.

It is not yet clear whether financial market problems will significantly slow the economy: many believe that the current episode is simply the downside of a normal credit cycle, that is, a natural corrective to several years of unusually easy credit conditions. On the other hand, some analysts identify market dynamics that may amplify the effects of financial shocks and have the potential to generate self-reinforcing, downward financial and economic spirals. The Federal Reserve has used its traditional tools to avert such an outcome: it has lowered short-term interest rates dramatically and injected billions of dollars into the banking system to support market liquidity and keep credit flowing. In addition, the Fed has expanded its sphere by making funds available to securities firms, which it does not regulate, and has provided funding to underwrite the rescue-through-acquisition of Bear Stearns, a leading investment bank. The duration of the current instability is in marked contrast to financial shocks of recent decades — stock market crashes, bond market disruptions, the 9/11 attacks — when the central bank was able to contain market problems quickly with little or no interruption of U.S. economic growth.

Depending on how soon normal market conditions are restored, and at what cost, policy makers may consider whether regulators have access to adequate information about market conditions, and whether currently unregulated market participants should be subjected to disclosure and reporting requirements. In addition, the social costs of failed financial speculation may be judged great enough to warrant new restrictions designed to lower the incidence of losses that have system-wide impacts or to put the markets and the economy in a better position to weather such shocks.

This chapter supplements CRS Report RL34 182, Financial Crisis? The Liquidity Crunch of August 2007, by Darryl Getter et al., which describes in greater detail the channels through which subprime problems cascaded through the financial system. This chapter focuses on the efforts of regulators to reduce stress to the markets.

Chapter 4 - After years of rapid appreciation, house prices barely rose in the second quarter of 2007, and many analysts expect price declines in many markets in the near future. There have already been large drops in house sales and residential investment (house building). Given the central role that the housing boom has played in the current economic expansion, many observers fear that a crash in the housing market will lead to an economy-wide recession. They are concerned that a fall in house prices could spill over into a decline in aggregate spending through four channels.

First, builders could respond to lower prices by reducing residential investment, an important component of gross domestic product (GDP). Second, since mortgages are backed by the value of the underlying house, a fall in prices could feed through to financial instability. Both of these effects have already been felt, with the rate of residential investment falling by double digits since mid-2006, and the entire financial sector undergoing a liquidity crunch triggered by problems with subprime mortgage-backed securities in August 2007.

Third, a fall in housing prices could lead to a decline in consumer spending through a negative "wealth effect." Some economists have argued that when house prices were rising, households responded to their greater housing wealth by increasing their consumption spending; were prices to fall, presumably the effect would be reversed. This effect is difficult to measure and faces some theoretical objections. For example, every housing transaction is composed of a buyer and seller. When house prices fall, sellers are made poorer but buyers are made wealthier, in the sense that they can now devote less of their income to mortgage payments and more to other consumption.

Fourth, the impending reset of mortgages to higher payments for many recent buyers could lead to a significant increase in the share of households suffering from financial distress. For some homeowners, a fall in prices would eliminate the option to refinance to avoid the distress. These homeowners may then be forced to reduce consumption spending in response.

Economic growth could decline in response to falling house prices through any of these four channels if all else remained equal. But it is possible that spending in other parts of the economy could rise and pick up the slack. And the government is not a neutral bystander when it comes to the path of aggregate spending. It can use expansionary fiscal or monetary policy to offset decreases to aggregate spending. The Federal Reserve has already responded to the housing and financial downturn by reducing short-term interest rates.

Most economic models suggest that a fall in prices in the range that has been predicted would not be enough to single-handedly cause a recession. But some observers think it may be enough to tip an already tepid economy into recession.

In: Financial Crisis in America ISBN 978-1-60692-191-3
Editor: Raymund T. Ovanhouser, pp. 1-45

Chapter 1

POLICY OPTIONS FOR THE HOUSING AND FINANCIAL MARKETS*

Congressional Budget Office

NOTES

All of the years referred to in this chapter are calendar years.

Some of the figures use shaded vertical bars to indicate periods of recession. (A recession extends from the peak of a business cycle to its trough.)

PREFACE

The housing and financial markets are in the midst of severe adjustments. House prices are falling rapidly, and they are expected to continue to fall. Mortgage foreclosures, particularly among subprime borrowers, have risen to record levels and are still rising. The financial markets are having severe difficulties adjusting to losses on mortgage-backed assets.

In response to a request from the Chairman of the Senate Budget Committee, the Congressional Budget Office (CBO) has examined the potential role of federal institutions and federal support in resolving the difficulties in the financial and

---

* Excerpted from CBO Paper dated April 11, 2008.

housing markets. This chapter updates and expands on issues raised in a January 2008 CBO paper, Options for Responding to Short-Term Economic Weakness.

Peter R. Orszag Director
April 2008

SECTION 1. INTRODUTION

Problems in the housing and mortgage markets have now spread to a broader array of financial markets. At this point, the nation faces a serious disruption to the functioning of its financial markets that could substantially impair economic activity in the near term. Since the end of the unusual housing boom from 2003 to early 2006, delinquencies and foreclosures on mortgages have risen, particularly on subprime adjustable-rate mortgage loans (ARMs), reflecting a retreat of house prices from unsustainable levels, the use of lax credit standards to make the loans, weak local economies, and in some cases, higher interest rates on ARMs whose interest rates had reset as scheduled in their loan contracts [1]. (Subprime loans are made to borrowers with low credit scores or other impairments to their credit histories.) The problems are not limited to subprime ARMs, however. Delinquencies have also risen for prime ARMs and on so-called alt-A mortgage loans, which are often made on the basis of little or no documentation of the borrower's income and may include low-downpayment loans, loans that are not for the owner's principal residence, interest-only loans, and loans whose balances rise over time. Because most mortgages are resold as mortgage-backed securities (MBSs), the rise in delinquencies has caused the value of MBSs to decline, in some cases quite sharply.

The problems in mortgage markets have spread to the wider financial markets for several reasons. Although highly uncertain, the number of bad mortgages and, consequently, losses on MBSs are expected to be large. The use of complex instruments to fund subprime lending, such as collateralized debt obligations (CDOs), also has made it difficult for participants in financial markets to identify the magnitude of the exposure of other participants to losses [2]. Moreover, a number of financial institutions borrowed heavily to finance their mortgage holdings, further increasing their risk exposure.

Those losses on mortgage assets, and the resulting contraction of the availability of credit to businesses and households, pose a significant threat to the pace of economic activity. Given the elevated uncertainty about their exposure to risk, financial institutions have tightened their lending standards and pulled back from all types of risky lending, preferring to conserve capital to guard against potential losses. Following a period in which the risk premium (the higher return required to compensate investors for assuming the risk of default) had been unusually low, the price of risk has risen, in some cases significantly. That pullback has extended to short-term lending between banks. In response, the Federal Reserve and some foreign central banks have intervened to provide large infusions of liquidity (that is, short-term financing) to keep financial markets from freezing up. Moreover, large numbers of foreclosures could trigger a downward spiral of house prices that could take them below what would be justified on the basis of normal relationships to income and production costs. Such a downward spiral would exacerbate the problems in the financial markets and could reduce consumption spending by reducing household wealth, increasing the likelihood and severity of a recession.

Policymakers have already taken steps to help the housing and financial markets cope with the aftereffects of the housing boom. In the wake of continuing weakness in those markets, though, additional actions have been proposed. (See Box 1.1 for a discussion of current federal housing policy.) Some of those actions would involve lenders (seeking to promote the modification of troubled mortgages), while others would expand the role of the federal government (providing or guaranteeing credit to mortgage markets). Such actions could help reduce the number of foreclosures, attenuating one source of downward pressure on house prices—although they would not address more important influences on prices. Many policy options, moreover, would significantly shift the risk involved in mortgage losses from current lenders and investors to taxpayers. (Policymakers are also considering new supervisory guidelines and regulations for financial institutions to address weaknesses that contributed to the problems in financial markets; this paper does not address those potential changes)

Whether additional policy interventions in the housing and mortgage markets are advisable depends in part on their objective:

- If the objective is to assist homeowners in distress, some of the policies seem likely to succeed, at least to some degree. Many policies intended to help homeowners may produce significant benefits for lenders as well. Avoiding some unintended effects will be virtually impossible because it is difficult to distinguish among homeowners who were victims of their poor judgment or of predatory lenders, those who overstretched their finances for purchasing investment properties, and those who exploited poor underwriting standards.

Box 1.1.

Federal Support for Housing

The government currently supports homeownership through various channels. The effects of that support in normal times are to increase the number of people who own their homes rather than rent and also to increase land prices, the average size and price of houses, and the proportion of wealth that is in the form of housing (as opposed to other forms of investment). There are also distributional consequences that favor homeowners relative to renters.

The federal government, through the Department of Housing and Urban Development (HUD), undertakes activities that reduce mortgage rates. The Federal Housing Administration (FHA) provides mortgage insurance on loans made by FHA-approved lenders that meet certain requirements. The Government National Mortgage Association (Ginnie Mae) provides liquidity to the secondary mortgage market by guaranteeing investors the timely payment of principal and interest on mortgage-backed securities backed by federally insured or guaranteed loans—mainly loans insured by the FHA or guaranteed by the Department of Veterans Affairs. Other guarantors or issuers of loans eligible as collateral for securities guaranteed by Ginnie Mae include the Department of Agriculture's Rural Housing Service and HUD's Office of Public and Indian Housing.

In addition, two privately owned government- sponsored enterprises (GSEs), Fannie Mae and Freddie Mac, provide capital to the mortgage markets by purchasing conforming mortgages, securitizing them, and charging a guarantee fee to investors. Although there is no explicit government guarantee of those securities, it is commonly perceived that the government would prevent a default. That implicit guarantee makes the cost of funds to the GSEs lower than it otherwise would be.[1]

The tax system is a major source of support for homeownership. Owner-occupied housing receives more favorable tax treatment from the federal government than most other privately held assets.[2] Much of the income generated by assets owned by businesses is subject to corporate or personal income taxes. However, the value of the services generated by owner-occupied housing is excluded from taxable income. Even so, owners may deduct certain expenses, such as interest paid on mortgage and home-equity loans and property tax payments. Most capital gains from the sale of an owner-occupied house are also tax-exempt.

The tax advantages for investing in one's home have been estimated to increase homeownership by between 2.5 percent and 5.4 percent, depending on people's income.[3] Furthermore, those advantages have been estimated to increase the amount of housing purchased by homeowners by between 5 percent and 21 percent, again depending on owners' income.

The study from which those estimates are derived assumes that additional land and other inputs for housing are available at no increase in cost, so none of the increase in purchases is absorbed in higher prices for houses and land. Those conditions seem more likely to exist on the outskirts of cities and in rural areas than in developed neighborhoods within large metropolitan areas, where limits on further development often exist. How much of the tax advantage is absorbed in higher prices inside metropolitan areas is disputed.[4]

[1] Congressional Budget Office, Federal Subsidies and the Housing GSEs (May 2001).

[2] See Congressional Budget Office, Taxing Capital Income: Effective Rates and Approaches to Reform (October 2005).

[3] Harvey S. Rosen, "Housing Decisions and the U.S. Income Tax," Journal of Public Economics, vol. 11, no. 1 (February 1979), pp. 1–23. Rosen reports the amount by which taxing homeownership like other investments would reduce the rate of homeownership and the amount of housing purchased. The estimates in Table 4 under Regime 2 have been converted above to increases from the tax advantage.

[4] Dennis R. Capozza, Richard K. Green, and Patric H. Hendershott, "Taxes, Mortgage Borrowing, and Residential Land Prices," in Henry J. Aaron and William G. Gale, eds., Economics of Fundamental Tax Reform (Washington, D.C.: Brookings Institution Press, 1996), pp. 171–198. Also see Donald Bruce and Douglas Holtz-Eakin, "Fundamental Tax Reform and Residential Housing," Journal of Housing and Economics, vol. 8, no. 4 (December 1999), pp. 249–271; and Jane G. Gravelle, The Flat Tax and Other Proposals: Effects on Housing, CRS Report for Congress 96-379 (April 29, 1996).

- If the objective is to avoid foreclosures and abandonment of properties, intervention might break a downward spiral in which foreclosures put houses on the market, pushing down house prices and producing more foreclosures. Although many analysts believe that house prices remain too high relative to people's incomes, such a spiral, without intervention, could reduce prices even below their long-run ratio to incomes and production costs
- If the objective is to arrest the decline in house prices, however, the policies are less likely to succeed. Perhaps the most important short-term influence on house prices is the elevated number of unoccupied houses for sale (the inventory overhang). That overhang is likely to remain until house prices fall enough to stimulate additional home sales. Put simply, none of the policies can (or presumably should) guarantee that house prices will stabilize in the near term. Furthermore, attempting to avoid (as opposed to attenuating) the market's necessary adjustments may not only be unrealistic, but even if it were to succeed, might ultimatelyserve only to delay the recovery of financial markets and impair the pace of economic activity.
- Finally, if the objective is to stabilize the overall economy, the policies under discussion will probably have only a limited effect because most of them are likely to exert only a modest influence directly on the housing market. (The Congressional Budget Office discussed policies more specifically related to general economic stimulus in a January 2008 paper, *Options for Responding to Short-Term Economic Weakness*.)

They might affect the economy indirectly, through their effects on consumer and investor confidence, though that is harder to predict

SECTION 2. THE CURRENT ECONOMIC SITUATION

The current economic situation is quite fragile. The turmoil in financial markets, the drop in house prices, and the rise in energy prices have combined to slow economic activity. Credit flows have dropped significantly as financial institutions have reduced their activity; nonfinancial firms face new constraints on their borrowing as well. The outlook for economic activity in 2008 has worsened, with private-sector payroll employment falling for the past four months and a growing number of economists indicating that the economy is in a recession. Nevertheless, both the tax rebates that will begin arriving late this spring (as part of the recently enacted economic stimulus package) and the Federal Reserve's reduction of short-term interest rates and injections of liquidity will help boost the economy. It remains unclear at this point whether the National Bureau of Economic Research will ultimately determine officially that there was a recession.

Economic Activity

Economic activity has slowed sharply since last summer. Annualized growth of real (inflation-adjusted) gross domestic product (GDP) declined to just 0.6 percent in the fourth quarter of 2007 from a robust 4.9 percent in the third quarter, and growth appears to have slowed even further this year. Employment fell by 300,000 between November 2007 and March 2008; such a decline in employment over several months strongly suggests that the economy has entered a recession. Real consumer spending has been essentially flat between November and February. Some of that weakness is related to high energy prices and slower gains in real disposable income, but some may also be a result of the effect of lower house prices on households' wealth. The pace of residential construction has been decreasing rapidly, and declining numbers of building permits for new construction suggest that those declines will persist in the near term. Business fixed investment also appears to have contracted in the first quarter, partly because financing for new projects has become more difficult to obtain. Offsetting some of that weakness has been strong growth in exports.

Concerns about inflation may constrain policymakers' efforts to stimulate the economy further. The sharp drop in the value of the dollar over the past year and the increase in a broad array of commodity prices have raised fears of higher inflation this year. Although most forecasters do not anticipate an increase in inflation during 2008, further monetary stimulus may set the stage for higher inflation in 2009.

House Prices and Mortgage Markets

House prices are falling across the country, with some of the steepest declines occurring in areas that had experienced some of the largest gains. Delinquencies and foreclosures on mortgages are also rising across the nation. Some states experiencing large price declines have also experienced high rates of delinquencies and foreclosures. However, prices of mortgage-backed securities have stabilized close to their recent lows, suggesting that investors' expectations about future losses on MBSs are no longer worsening.

House Prices. Prices for houses have fallen sharply since their peak in the middle of 2006, and the decline appears to be accelerating. A number of indexes are available to track prices; each has its limitations, but together they give a sense of trends. One measure, the S&P/CaseShiller national price index for single-family homes, was down by about 9 percent in the fourth quarter of 2007 as compared with the fourth quarter of 2006, after a 4.6 percent decline in the year ending in the third quarter of 2007. In real terms, the decline last year was almost 12 percent. Rapid declines in house prices continued in January: A narrower S&P/Case-Shiller index for 20 cities (reported monthly) fell by 10.7 percent in the year ending in January, while the monthly index for the S&P/Case-Shiller index for 10 cities was down by 11.4 percent over the same period. Those trends are generally confirmed by a third price index, published by Radar Logic, a real estate and data-analysis firm. Another widely used index, the purchase-only index published by the Office of Federal Housing Enterprise Oversight (OFHEO), did not begin to decline until May 2007. The difference between the movement of that index and the movement of the other indexes may reflect the fact that OFHEO's index excludes homes with nonconforming (for example, subprime) mortgages and thus omits the parts of the market that have seen the greatest difficulties in recent months [1].

The outlook for house prices is highly uncertain, but prices are likely to continue to fall, on average, at least through the end of 2008. Expectations of such a decline are widespread. Prices implied by futures contracts, for example, indicate that market participants expect large additional drops in house prices. Futures contracts on the S&P/Case-Shiller index for 10 cities project a decline of about 13 percent in nominal prices over the coming year and 16 percent by November 2009 (see Figure 2.1) [2].

Another measure, based on Radar Logic's composite index of 25 cities, projects declines of 13 percent over the next year and 21 percent over the next three years. (However, those indexes may not indicate what is expected to happen to house prices nationwide.) Private forecasters and investment firms also expect significant declines in nominal house prices. Macroeconomic Advisers, for its March 2008 forecast, assumed a 5.6 percent fall in prices from the end of 2007 to mid- 2009. Global Insight, another economic consulting firm, projects a 12 percent decline over the same period in its April forecast.

Delinquencies and Foreclosures of Mortgages. National delinquency and foreclosure rates are rising for both prime and subprime loans, particularly for adjustable-rate loans [3]. In the fourth quarter of 2007, 17.3 percent of all subprime loans were delinquent, up from 13.3 percent at the end of 2006. For subprime ARMs, 20 percent were delinquent in the fourth quarter of 2007, up from 14.4 percent in the fourth quarter of 2006. The delinquency rate on prime ARMs has also risen, from 3.4 percent at the end of 2006 to 5.5 percent at the end of last year (see Figure 2.2). In addition, the share of subprime ARMs entering foreclosure more than tripled, increasing from an average of 1.5 percent in 2004 and 2005 to 5.3 percent in the fourth quarter of 2007 (see Figure 2.3). Although the rate of delinquency on fixed- rate subprime loans has also grown, it is still much lower and has risen more slowly than that on subprime ARMs.

Rates of foreclosure are particularly high in areas experiencing economic weakness or large declines in house prices. Of the 10 states with the highest percentage of loans in foreclosure, 5 are among the 10 states with the largest declines in house prices.

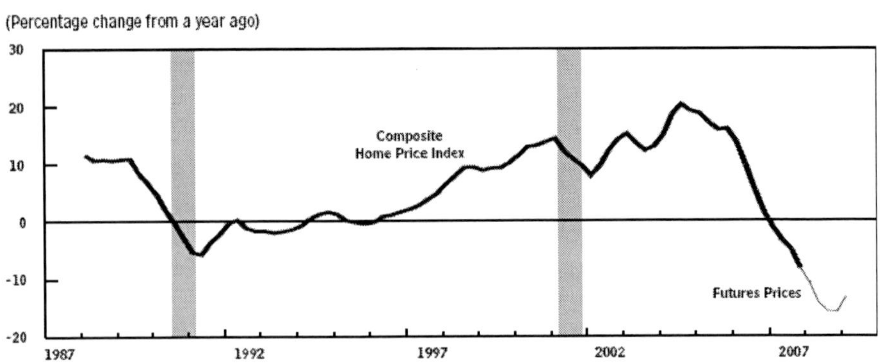

Sources: Congressional Budget Office; Bloomberg; Chicago Mercantile Exchange.

Note: The S&P/Case-Shiller 10-city composite home price index tracks price changes in 10 metropolitan areas on the basis of a house's previous sale. Data are quarterly and are plotted through the first quarter of 2009. The figure includes implied values from futures prices for the second quarter of 2008 through the first quarter of 2009.

Figure 2.1. S&P/Case-Shiller 10-City Composite Home Price Index and Implied Values from Futures Prices.

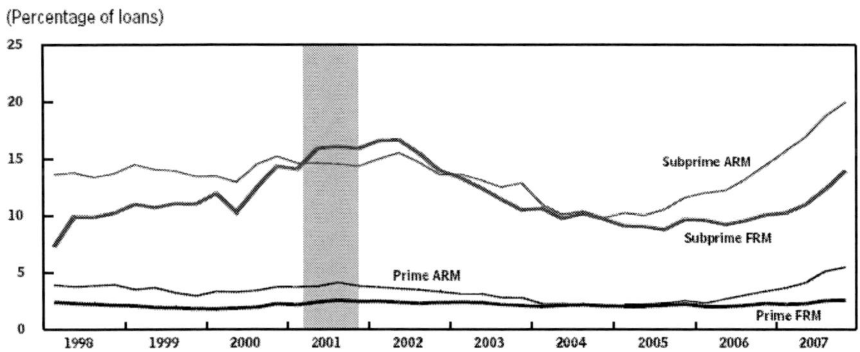

Sources: Congressional Budget Office; Mortgage Bankers Association.
Notes: Data are quarterly and are plotted through the fourth quarter of 2007.
ARM = adjustable-rate mortgage; FRM = fixed-rate mortgage. Subprime loans are made to borrowers with low credit scores or other impairments to their credit histories.

Figure 2.2. Mortgage Delinquencies.

Interest Rates on Mortgage Loans. Mortgage interest rates continue to reflect the heightened aversion to risk in financial markets. The interest rate on 30-year conforming mortgages, which can be securitized by the government-sponsored enterprises (GSEs) Fannie Mae and Freddie Mac, has fallen below 6 percent (see Figure 2.4). Although that rate is about one-half of a percentage point lower than it was in the past two years, the spread between that mortgage rate and the rate on seven- year Treasury notes—a measure of the market's current preference for the safest and most liquid collateral—continued to widen earlier this year [4].

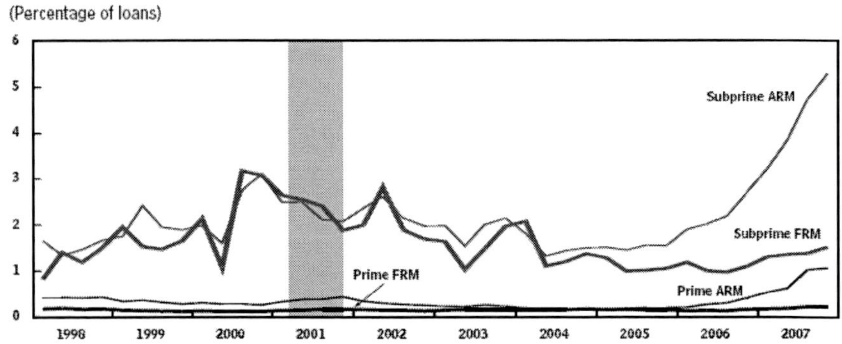

Sources: Congressional Budget Office; Mortgage Bankers Association.

Notes: Data are quarterly and are plotted through the fourth quarter of 2007.

ARM = adjustable-rate mortgage; FRM = fixed-rate mortgage. Subprime loans are made to borrowers with low credit scores or other impairments to their credit histories.

Figure 2.3. Mortgage Foreclosures Initiated.

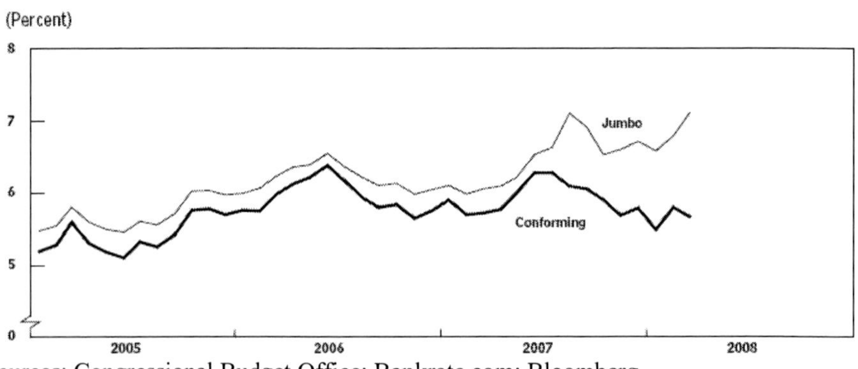

Sources: Congressional Budget Office; Bankrate.com; Bloomberg.

Notes: Data are monthly and are plotted through March 2008. Jumbo loans exceed the loan limits of Fannie Mae and Freddie Mac.

Figure 2.4. Rates on 30-Year Mortgages.

Moreover, the rate on jumbo loans (those that exceed Fannie Mae's and Freddie Mac's loan limits) has moved up sharply since early February and currently is about 2 percentage points higher than the rate on conforming mortgages.

Initial rates for adjustable-rate mortgages, by contrast, dropped sharply earlier this year. In addition, the benchmark interest rate typically used for resetting the interest rate on subprime ARMs—the six-month Libor rate—has fallen significantly in the past few months and is now back down to levels last seen in the beginning of 2005 (see Figure 2.5) [5]. That decline reflects the large amount of liquidity added by the Federal Reserve and other central banks in response to the turmoil in financial markets. As a result, the risk that resetting interest rates on subprime ARMs will lead to a substantial number of additional mortgage defaults has fallen.

Prices of Mortgage-Backed Securities. The very high rates of delinquency on recent subprime mortgage loans surprised investors last year, who pulled back sharply from potential exposure to such lending in their investments during the summer. Lenders have virtually stopped making new subprime loans. Trading of existing subprime MBSs has diminished because of uncertainty about their value, particularly in view of investors' loss of confidence in the securities' credit ratings. Indeed, price declines on those MBSs have been striking, especially for subprime MBSs that were issued more recently and whose mortgages have experienced unusually high rates of defaults.

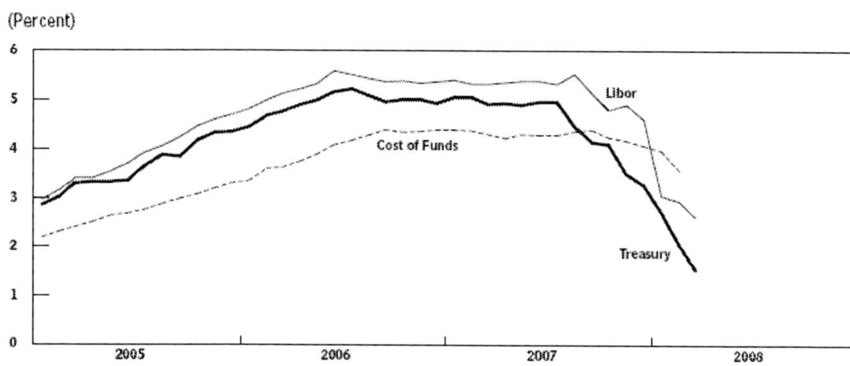

Sources: Congressional Budget Office; Bloomberg.

Notes: The indexes shown are for the one-year constant maturity Treasury bill, the six-month Libor, and the 11th District Federal Home Loan Bank's cost of funds.

Data are monthly. The Libor and Treasury-bill rates are plotted through March 2008; the cost of funds rate is through February 2008.

Figure 2.5. Popular Adjustable-Rate-Mortgage Indexes.

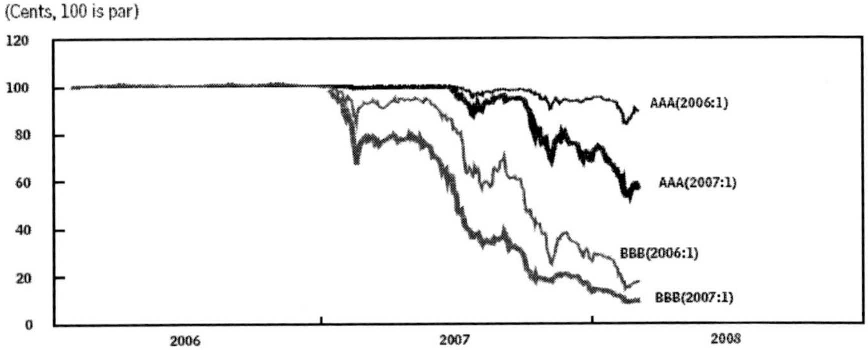

Source: Congressional Budget Office based on data from the Markit Group.

Notes: Prices are inferred from the Markit ABX.HE index for the BBB (next to the lowest investment grade) and AAA (highest investment grade) tranches of mortgage-backed securities. The 2006:1 vintage reflects mortgages available for securitization from July 19, 2005, to January 5, 2006. The 2007:1 vintage reflects mortgages available for securitization from July 19, 2006, to January 5, 2007.

Data are daily and are plotted through March 28, 2008.

Subprime loans are made to borrowers with low credit scores or other impairments to their credit histories.

Figure 2.6. Inferred Prices of Subprime Mortgage Tranches.

The values of subprime mortgage securities (MBS tranches) can be inferred from ABX indexes related to those securities [6]. Those indexes are available for MBS tranches with different initial credit ratings [7]. As of late March 2008, the index for subprime MBSs issued in the second half of 2006 and initially rated BBB was 9 cents on the dollar, and the index for those initially rated AAA was 57 cents on the dollar (see Figure 2.6) [8]. In both cases, index values a year ago were closer to 100 cents on the dollar. For subprime MBSs issued earlier, in the last half of 2005, prices have not fallen as much. Prices ranged from 17 cents on the dollar for the BBB-rated securities to 88 cents for the AAA-rated securities.

Financial Markets

The broader financial markets have also experienced significant turmoil recently. Lending in some markets remains depressed, as financial institutions continue to struggle to find ways of adequately dealing with losses on their leveraged financing of very risky mortgage loans and other risky assets [9]. Consequently, the risk of a systemic crisis in financial markets spurred by the collapse of one or more important financial institutions or markets remains elevated.

Credit Markets. Interest rates on investment-grade corporate bonds have remained relatively steady, but because the yield on the 10-year Treasury note has fallen sharply since last June, the interest rate spread has widened. Investors' tolerance for risk appears to have decreased as yields on below-investment-grade corporate securities have risen, particularly those with the lowest credit ratings (see Figure 2.7). Issuances of new corporate debt have fallen noticeably, as have those for asset-backed corporate paper. The interbank market for short-term loans also continues to experience problems; despite efforts by the Federal Reserve and some foreign central banks to shore up this market, the spread between the three-month Libor rate and the expected federal funds rate has moved upward recently (see Figure 2.8). [10].

The Potential for Mortgage Losses. The ultimate volume of defaulted mortgages, which will affect both homeowners and investors, depends in part on the overall performance of the economy and on the size of the remaining gap between house prices and sustainable levels. A severe recession would result in larger mortgage losses than a mild recession or a short period of slow growth because a substantial recession would further depress house prices and homeowners' ability to finance their mortgages. Similarly, to the extent that house prices have farther to fall, losses will be larger than if prices have already declined to close to sustainable levels.

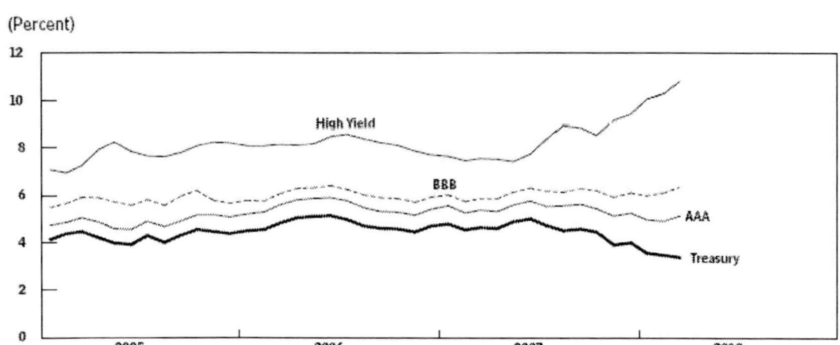

Sources: Congressional Budget Office; Bloomberg.

Note: Data are monthly and are plotted through March 2008.

Figure 2.7. Yields on 10-Year Bonds.

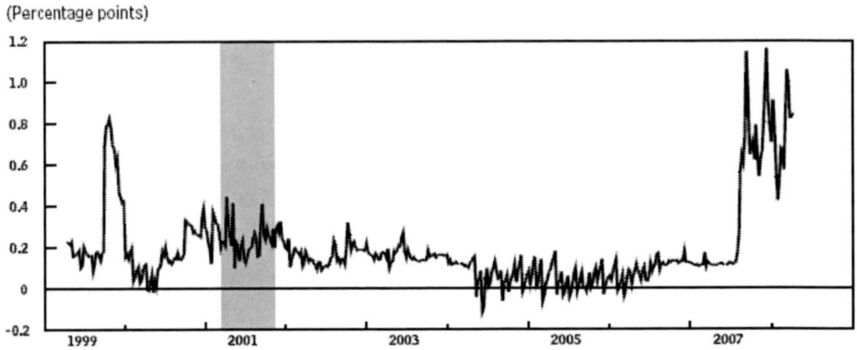

Sources: Congressional Budget Office; Bloomberg.

Note: Data are weekly and are plotted through April 4, 2008. The expected federal funds rate is based on the futures price two months ahead.

Figure 2.8. Spread Between the Three-Month Libor Rate and the Expected Federal Funds Rate.

The wide range of estimates of losses quoted in the media is due in part to the great uncertainty about the outlook for the overall economy and the ultimate level of house prices. With sluggish but continued economic growth or a mild recession, as well as further declines of roughly 10 percent to 15 percent in average national house prices by mid- 200 9, the value of all mortgages that will enter foreclosure without further policy action could be about $500 billion to $600 billion over the next two years [11]. The ultimate losses on those mortgages will be smaller, possibly in the range of $100 billion to $250 billion, because some of the houses will not end up being repossessed. Also, considerable value will probably be recovered from new agreements worked out between borrowers and lenders and from foreclosure sales, for example. However, the recovery rate will most likely be lower than it has been in the past, particularly in some areas of the ountry, and sales of foreclosed properties may take several years to materialize.

Financial institutions worldwide have already recognized about $230 billion in losses from the broader credit problem that began last year in subprime loans [12]. The International Monetary Fund recently estimated that total losses to all financial institutions around the world would approach $1 trillion, with more than half of that coming from residential mortgages and the rest coming from commercial mortgages, credit card loans, and automobile loans, among others. That amount would represent a notable loss of capital among the world's financial institutions, enough to significantly reduce the availability of credit.

Risks to the Financial System. The existence of substantial unrealized losses and uncertainty about which institutions are exposed to such losses may further impede the flow of credit in the United States and abroad. The possibility of large undisclosed losses has driven investors away from both the long- and short-term obligations of financial institutions. For the same reasons, financial institutions have become increasingly wary of lending to one another. In addition, institutions with assets of uncertain value on their balance sheets are likely to find it difficult to raise capital until the true value of those assets has been recognized because new investors will not want to share possible losses with current shareholders.

So far, problems in financial markets have not become severe enough to create a complete breakdown in the credit system. Such a breakdown could occur if lenders felt that they could not determine the risk they would be taking by lending to other entities: In that case, lending would stop, at least for a time. In such a scenario, even creditworthy borrowers could find credit difficult to obtain. Markets are still able to distinguish between those institutions that are creditworthy and those that are less so, as evidenced by sharp differences in the movement of stock prices of different banks. However, the near collapse of another major financial institution would further undermine the market's confidence and could severely cripple the financial system. That possibility is why the Federal Reserve has taken extraordinary actions to prevent such a failure.

Government Actions to Support Economic Activity and Stabilize Financial Markets

Both monetary and fiscal policymakers have taken significant steps to contain the economic damage caused by the turmoil in financial markets, but it remains unclear whether even those actions will prove sufficient to avoid a major recession. Fiscal policymakers have adopted an economic stimulus package whose effects should begin to manifest themselves late this spring. In addition, and perhaps more important, the Federal Reserve has taken extraordinary measures in addition to rapidly reducing the federal funds rate. In essence, the Federal Reserve has used its unmatched credit rating and large lending capacity to serve as an intermediary among financial institutions.

Fiscal Stimulus

In February, lawmakers enacted the Economic Stimulus Act of 2008 [13]. That law provides tax rebates of up to $600 to individual filers, up to $1,200 for couples, and $300 per child. In addition, the law allows businesses to take additional deductions for accelerated depreciation and immediate expensing of capital purchases. That legislation will add an estimated $152 billion to the federal deficit in 2008 and another $16 billion in 2009. Overall, the Congressional Budget Office estimates that the law's provisions will add about 0.7 percentage points to the growth of real GDP in 2008 [14].

Actions by the Federal Reserve

The Federal Reserve instituted several actions in March to quell a crisis of confidence in the markets. The most extraordinary of those were creating a Primary Dealer Credit Facility and facilitating the acquisition of Bear Stearns by J.P. Morgan Chase.

The Primary Dealer Credit Facility allows all primary dealers to borrow funds overnight directly from the Federal Reserve [15]. Previously, that privilege was extended only to deposit-taking commercial banks. That step implies that the Federal Reserve is taking responsibility for ensuring liquidity not just to commercial banks, but also to a much broader swath of the financial market. In less unsettled times, ensuring that commercial banks have enough liquidity would be sufficient because those banks could then lend to the rest of the market. The need to provide liquidity directly to primary dealers is an indication of the breakdown of the usual flow of credit.

In another such indication, during the week ending Friday, March 14, other financial institutions lost confidence in Bear Stearns, the nation's fifth-largest investment bank, creating a potential liquidity crisis. Over that weekend, the Federal Reserve was involved in negotiations for J.P. Morgan's acquisition of Bear Stearns. The Federal Reserve lent $29 billion to J.P. Morgan against a portfolio of $30 billion of Bear Stearns' less liquid assets. In the event of losses on those assets, J.P. Morgan would be responsible for the first $1 billion in losses, and the Federal Reserve Bank of New York—and ultimately taxpayers—would absorb any remaining losses. (Taxpayers would be involved because any such losses would diminish the amount of the Federal Reserve's surplus that is turned over to the Treasury and recorded as federal revenues.)

The Federal Reserve has also continued to use its conventional tools. At the March 18 Federal Open Market Committee meeting, the federal funds target rate was reduced by 75 basis points, to 2.25 percent. The spread between the discount rate and the federal funds target rate was reduced to 25 basis points [16]. In its continuing effort to reduce strains in financial markets, the central bank has also enhanced its mechanisms for lending funds to financial institutions against illiquid collateral (investments that cannot be readily converted into cash). The Federal Reserve enlarged the amount of funds available to be lent under the twice-monthly Term Auction Facility from $30 billion to $50 billion. It also announced that it would lend up to an additional $100 billion to primary dealers in the form of 28-day repurchase agreements— another step to provide liquidity to that market.

Following those actions by the Federal Reserve and other central banks, short-term interest rates have fallen, but the perceived riskiness of the interbank loan market has not changed greatly. The spread between the cost of three-month Libor funding and the expected federal funds rate over the same period did narrow, but only modestly, and that spread remains well above typical levels.

SECTION 3. POLICY OPTIONS

Policymakers have already taken steps to help the housing and mortgage markets cope with the effects of the end of the housing boom, and additional actions are under consideration. Some of those actions involve new ways of promoting the modification of troubled mortgages, while others involve having the federal government directly provide or guarantee credit to mortgage markets. Such actions would help avoid foreclosures and ease the downward pressure on house prices, helping the market adjust in a more orderly manner.1 Many policy options, however, would also significantly shift the risk involved in mortgage losses from current lenders and investors to taxpayers. (Policymakers are also considering new supervisory guidelines and regulations for financial institutions to address weaknesses that contributed to the problems in financial markets. Those issues are not addressed in this paper)

Considerations for Policymakers

Several possible short-term goals could motivate policy interventions:

- Assist borrowers who unwittingly overcommitted their income to mortgage payments. Many of those borrowers may have lacked sufficient financial sophistication to understand the nature of the risks they were undertaking. A related objective could be to lessen the social costs of having large numbers of people move out of their houses and into others.

- Avoid excessive declines in asset prices—house prices as well as prices of mortgage-related assets. That task may be very difficult to achieve because of the near impossibility of determining fair values in current markets. House prices, in particular, are expected to continue to fall for at least a year because of the overhang of unoccupied units, and such an adjustment is necessary to allow the housing market to function again. However, there is a risk that the price adjustment may get out of hand in some areas, as forced or panic selling causes prices to decline too much.
- Reduce the costs of loan modification, refinancing, or foreclosure.
- Stimulate the economy as a whole in order to avoid or mitigate a recession. The housing market's troubles affect the rest of the economy by reducing activity in the housing market itself, by decreasing homeowners' wealth (which gives them less collateral for borrowing and tends to constrain their spending), and by contributing to problems in financial markets.
- Support credit markets to mitigate turbulence in financial markets. Financial markets play a crucial role in a modern economy, and intervening to keep them working smoothly may help mitigate broader costs to the economy.
- Facilitate the cleaning up of balance sheets. The availability of credit to financial institutions, and hence to businesses and households that borrow from those institutions, could be limited if assets on their balance sheets are difficult to value. Moreover, institutions will have greater difficulty raising capital because potential investors will not know what they are buying and will not wish to share losses on current assets with existing shareholders.

Those goals are not always mutually compatible, and different policy interventions may fulfill some objectives but not others. For instance, supporting financial institutions in difficulty to prevent broader problems in financial markets may conflict with the goal of recognizing losses as quickly as possible to clean up balance sheets. Keeping homeowners in their houses may delay the necessary revaluation of the housing stock.

Whatever policymakers' goals, a key consideration is to avoid policies that distort incentives excessively. For example, homeowners who otherwise are capable of making their payments might take on additional debt or miss mortgage payments in order to create an impression of financial difficulty if doing so qualified them for mortgage assistance. Pressuring lenders to modify existing contracts may appear to benefit current borrowers, but such action could also ultimately raise interest rates on future credit transactions and thereby harm future borrowers.

One contribution that federal policymakers can make is to encourage a standard package for restructuring mortgages, including such things as how to determine what monthly payment the borrower can manage and how to distribute losses among first- and second-lien holders. Such a standard package, if it is sufficiently realistic, could be useful even if it is voluntary and even if it does not provide any federal monetary support. In that case, it could reduce the number of decisions that need to be made in a restructuring, speeding up the process. In addition, having a standard for restructuring could help gain assent from the various stakeholders—including second- lien holders and holders of low-ranked MBS tranches. Having rules for the restructuring is essential if there is to be a federal monetary commitment.

Loan Restructuring

A number of proposals aim to facilitate the restructuring of existing mortgages to help homeowners avoid foreclosure and stay in their current residences. Loan restructurings fall into two broad but not mutually exclusive categories: reducing the principal of a mortgage and changing the terms of a mortgage. A goal of many of the proposals is to make loan repayment more attractive to borrowers while providing lenders with a greater return than that realized from foreclosure (see Box 3.1) [2].

Impediments to Voluntary Loan Restructuring. There are several legal and economic reasons that lenders may be reluctant to use loan restructurings to resolve mortgage repayment problems. Legal impediments arise in cases in which borrowers have a second mortgage or have a mortgage that has been securitized (that is, sold as a part of a mortgage-backed security). Economic impediments include imperfect information about borrowers and the perverse incentives that can be created for some borrowers by restructuring the loans of other borrowers.

Legal Impediments. One impediment to restructuring mortgages occurs when the borrower has a second mortgage. During the housing boom, a significant percentage of borrowers took on second mortgages. In February 2008, about 30 percent of subprime and alt-A loans had second mortgages [3] The holders of the first mortgage and the second mortgage often have substantially different interests and bargaining powers. Given the decline in house prices, the market value of many second mortgages has often disappeared, and they would be worthless under foreclosure.

Box 3.1. The Costs of Foreclosure

With house prices falling in most areas of the country, some mortgage lenders are likely to suffer substantial losses from defaults and foreclosures. Estimates of the losses when a house is repossessed range from 30 percent to 60 percent of the value of the loan.1 About half of those losses occur prior to the foreclosure process—that is, from the decline in the price of the house, missed interest payments, and unpaid property taxes.2 The other half of the losses reflect the costs of preparing the house for sale (which includes lost interest payments during the time it is on the market); the expense of selling it; and, if the house is foreclosed, associated legal expenses. Those latter costs are the primary costs of foreclosure itself. (Any missed loan payments and any decline in the price of the house before foreclosure are not considered costs of foreclosure.) Lenders typically are unable to recover such losses. The losses will be realized regardless of whether the homeowner leaves voluntarily or through foreclosure.

In addition to those costs, in foreclosure the lender loses the opportunity to share in the potential appreciation of the house. Although it is difficult to value that opportunity, a reasonable expectation might be 3 percent of the value of the house.3 That calculation implies that 50 percent to 55 percent of the loss to lenders might be avoided under alternatives to foreclosure—in other words, about 20 percent to 25 percent of the outstanding balance of the mortgage.

[1] That range comes from Charles Capone, Providing Alternatives to Mortgage Foreclosure: A Report to Congress (Department of Housing and Urban Development, March 1996). An estimate in March 2008 by consultant organization Clayton Holdings set the average loss from delinquencies on first-lien subprime and alt-A loans at about 40 percent. A third estimate, which used a 50 percent loss for all mortgages, comes from David Greenlaw and others, "Leverage Losses: Lessons from the Mortgage Market Meltdown" (U.S. Monetary Policy Forum Conference Draft, February 2008).

[2] Amy Crew Cutts and William Merrill, "Interventions in Mortgage Default: Policies and Practices to Prevent Home Loss and Lower Costs" (Freddie Mac Working Paper, March 2008).

[3] The 3 percent estimate is based on the price of an at-themoney call option that expires after five years on an asset with an expected price decline of 1.5 percent per year and a volatility of 6 percent.

Second-lien holders in such situations would seek to avoid foreclosure or a short sale because either would eliminate the potential for their loans to regain value if prices recovered in the future [4]. (In effect, second- lien holders have a call option on the value of the house—if the value goes down, they are not subject to further losses, but they will gain if prices recover)

To avoid the costly foreclosure process, the first-lien holder may have an interest in reducing the payment obligation of the borrower or permitting a short sale. Because the priority of liens generally follows the order in which they are recorded, for a refinancing lender to have the senior lien, a second lien must also be repaid or resubordinated. The second-lien holders, however, may withhold their consent to resubordination (if required) or threaten foreclosure to bargain with both the homeowner and the first-lien holder. In many cases, the ability to help borrowers having difficulty may first require coordination and agreement between the holders of the first and second mortgages [6].

A second impediment concerns securitization. In some cases, complex interests inherent in securitization could impede the ability of a loan servicer to modify loans that belong to a securitized pool. To receive favorable tax and accounting treatment, the special-purpose entities that issue MBSs must avoid becoming active managers in a technical sense defined by the tax laws. Many mitigation efforts are permissible under current law because the Internal Revenue Service (IRS) and the Chief Accountant of the Securities and Exchange Commission (SEC) determined that as long as servicers follow a certain set of industry guidelines (the ASF Framework), their actions would not jeopardize the tax and accounting status of the special-purpose entities [7]. Proposals for mitigation efforts outside the ASF Framework, however, must address how to maintain the current tax and accounting treatment.

In addition, contractual terms may sometimes restrict servicers' actions [8]. For example, pooling and servicing agreements may prevent the exchange of an existing loan for a new loan, such as one that allows participation in equity appreciation in exchange for modification of existing terms. Most recent pooling and servicing agreements give servicers authority to modify securitized loans if that action is in the interest of maximizing the value of the loan pool, but some agreements may be more restrictive. Pooling and servicing agreements can be amended with the consent of investors. However, investors in different tranches of mortgage-backed securities share losses unequally, which may limit servicers' ability to obtain permission to engage in additional mitigation actions.

The Congress is considering various proposals to protect servicers of securitized loans who agree to restructure mortgages (through modifications, partial discharge of principal, or short sales)—if the servicers believe that such restructuring will increase the value received on the loans over that which would be received through foreclosure [9]. Proponents argue that by providing servicers with legal certainty, the proposals would increase the number of mortgages that servicers chose to restructure. Opponents argue that the proposals are unnecessary because servicers already are protected if they compare all of the loss-mitigation options and choose the one that maximizes the return to the loan pool.

Economic Impediments. Lenders may be unwilling to adjust a loan's balance, despite the potential benefits, for two reasons. First, although some borrowers walk away from their homes when the home's value drops below the mortgage balance, more do not.10 There is no workable way to distinguish between those types of borrowers ahead of time, and the cost of reworking every distressed loan would be far greater than dealing with the foreclosure expenses of only those borrowers who walked away. Moreover, offering a reduction of principal to "distressed" homeowners might encourage people who were otherwise capable of making payments to attempt to qualify for the benefit by taking on additional debt or missing several mortgage payments to suggest financial difficulties. Second, lenders would have no confidence that a borrower whose mortgage was rewritten would not choose to walk away if house prices fell even lower. Although Federal Reserve Chairman Ben Bernanke has urged loan servicers to consider reducing the principal on outstanding loans, voluntary reductions are likely to be rare.

Proposals to Facilitate Changing Mortgage Terms. A number of plans would keep a borrower's mortgage principal unchanged but lower the monthly payment for a possibly limited time. Under those plans, lenders would voluntarily negotiate such payment forbearance on a caseby-case basis. Most proposals have focused on preventing an increase in the interest rate on adjustable-rate subprime loans that are scheduled for their first interest rate reset in the next two years. (The decline in short- term interest rates engineered by the Federal Reserve has sharply reduced the size of any increase in initial resets and may even lower rates for some ARM borrowers this year.) Some proposals would lower payments both for adjustable-rate loans even when their rates have not changed and for fixed-rate loans. Lenders would find such proposals more attractive if borrowers' missed payments were added to their principal. If lenders bear the cost of the lower payments, such proposals are in many ways similar to reducing the loan principal.

Rate Freezes on Adjustable-Rate Loans. The Administration reached a voluntary agreement with some lenders in December 2007 to freeze interest rates for generally five years on certain types of subprime loans.[11] Eligibility is limited to subprime borrowers who face an initial adjustment to their mortgage interest rate between January 1, 2008, and July 31, 2010, and meet the eligibility criteria of the ASF Framework (see reference 7). Although lenders would bear losses from the lower-than-agreed-upon interest rate, those losses might not be recognized immediately (unlike a principal reduction), depending on the accounting treatment. With the reduction in short-term interest rates, this freeze may have little impact in the coming year but may be more important when economic activity recovers and those rates rise [12].

Other proponents have offered broader freezes. Some proposals would freeze rates on all subprime loans for up to seven years regardless of borrowers' equity or payment history. Others would go beyond subprime loans and would freeze rates for all adjustable-rate loans. Although broader plans would help more needy borrowers, they also would offer a windfall to borrowers who were not in difficulty at the expense of the holders of those mortgages. Convincing lenders to freeze scheduled adjustments of interest rates for a wider range of borrowers without adequate compensation would probably require some compulsion or financial inducements from the federal government. To the extent that lenders perceived a broad-scale freeze as a significant change in contractual terms (which is more likely under a compulsory change), the result would probably be higher interest rates on mortgages and other credit transactions in the future. In particular, lenders would require some compensation to protect against the risk that policymakers would again freeze interest rates or intervene in some other way.

If the goal of interest rate freezes is to help borrowers remain in their homes, the success would depend in part on their net equity in the homes as well as other factors, such as the borrowers' ties to their homes and costs of moving. In the current environment of lower short-term interest rates, borrowers' equity in their homes may be a more important determinant of the likelihood of foreclosures and walking away from homes with burdensome monthly payments [13]. As long as the market value of the house exceeds the mortgage balance, a borrower has an ability and an incentive to sell or refinance the home rather than walk away, even when payments are perceived to be onerous.

Other Ways to Lower Mortgage Payments. Some proposals would mandate that lenders allow borrowers to lower their payments in exchange for a greater stake in the equity of the home or an increase in the mortgage balance. That is, the restructuring would substitute a shared appreciation loan or a negative amortization loan for the current loan. A shared appreciation loan entitles lenders

to receive a share of any increase in the value of a house in exchange for giving the borrower a below-market interest rate (thus lowering the monthly payment) [14]. Borrowers who do not have much initial equity in their homes are better off with the lower payments when house prices decline. Negative amortization or deferred-interest loans offer lower payments and capitalize the shortfall into a larger principal balance.

Borrowers have the option to make a minimum payment, one that is less than the original interest due. The amount that the payment falls short of the interest owed is added to the principal. Negative amortization loans might make sense for borrowers expecting their income to increase in the future, but such loans would merely defer problems for borrowers whose loan amounts exceeded what they could afford in the longer term. Some proposals to modify bankruptcy law also would allow changing mortgage terms.

Proposals to Facilitate the Reduction of Mortgage Balances

Proposals to reduce mortgage balances aim to help people stay in their homes, which may also help stabilize the current housing market. Those proposals provide incentives to dissuade homeowners whose loan balance is greater than the current market value of their homes from walking away from their mortgages when they can afford to pay them [15]. Studies have shown that the greater the shortfall between the value of a house and the amount of a borrower's mortgage, the greater the likelihood that the borrower will default on his or her mortgage [16]. Under certain conditions, lenders might prefer to voluntarily rewrite a mortgage for the current value of a home rather than have a borrower walk away, especially in a declining housing market. Rewriting the principal balance of the loan avoids a costly foreclosure in a depressed market and gives the borrower an incentive to continue repaying the loan.

Determining the fair value of a house, and hence the appropriate write-down of the mortgage principal, may be difficult in the current circumstances, however. The national housing market is not likely to stabilize for some time, and house prices will probably continue to fall. That process of moving to stability is not likely to proceed evenly—some regions experienced larger price increases and building expansions than others, and thus they may take longer to adjust. In some neighborhoods, home prices may even dip below levels needed to stabilize the market when there are a large number of foreclosures or panic sales.

Some proposals involve changing federal bankruptcy law to allow bankruptcy judges to restructure certain mortgages on principal residences under Chapter 13, by limiting a mortgage to the current value of a home, for instance, or by changing the terms of a loan. Under current law, Chapter 13 halts foreclosure proceedings by lenders, giving homeowners an opportunity to restructure their financial situation. While Chapter 13 gives courts leeway to adjust many financial obligations, it currently does not generally allow the terms of a mortgage on a principal residence to be modified [17]. Changing that provision of Chapter 13 would allow bankruptcy courts to treat mortgages on a primary residence in the same way as secured debts on other items, such as motor vehicles, vacation homes, investment properties, and personal businesses. (In practice, bankruptcy judges seldom restructure mortgages on vacation or investment properties.)

Allowing a bankruptcy court to modify the amount or terms of mortgages changes incentives for both borrowers and lenders. It gives borrowers an incentive to file for bankruptcy as a way to lower their mortgage payments and avert foreclosure. Consequently, lenders would have a greater incentive to restructure loans voluntarily. Lenders would also have a greater incentive to be more prudent in making loans, which could help avoid future excesses in the mortgage markets. In doing so, lenders might raise mortgage rates, particularly for high-risk borrowers, to offset any expected greater losses from loan modifications in bankruptcy. However, there are divergent views on how much mortgage interest rates would rise [18]. The increase may be limited in part because lenders might also change other lending terms to reduce their exposure to losses. Changing the bankruptcy law could also add to the caseload of the bankruptcy court system [19].

Federal Assistance to Participants in the Mortgage Market

Although private participants in mortgage and financial markets will probably try to address the problems in those markets on their own, some plans would have the government (that is, taxpayers) contribute resources to encourage certain types of outcomes. Indeed, the government has already begun to do so, through initiatives involving the Federal Reserve and agencies involved in housing. Proposals for increasing that intervention revolve around extending federal credit or insurance to new and existing borrowers or mortgage lenders. The existing regulatory framework permits some expansion of federal housing and banking agencies' activity without Congressional action. Alternatively, a new agency could be created for the purpose, as it was during the Depression and in the thrift crisis of the 1 980s. Finally, some proposals would rely on state and local governments.

If policymakers conclude that some commitment of resources is appropriate, they also will have to determine who should benefit from such resources. Acquiring loans in order to refinance them would directly assist borrowers and could help them avert foreclosure, thus limiting the likelihood of a downward spiral in house prices. Purchases or guarantees that were targeted to relieve lenders or mortgage pools of the risk from the most troubled loans would provide investors with more confidence in mortgage-backed securities and financial intermediaries. Providing credit to lenders without intervening in mortgage arrangements would help them keep their doors open and could be used as an incentive for lenders to work out a solution for their at-risk borrowers.

All such proposals, however, have downsides (beyond their budgetary costs). In the short term, extending credit to borrowers or lenders in a precarious financial position might encourage borrowers who were able to pay their debts to stop paying them in order to qualify for federal assistance. In the long run, some observers are concerned that expanding the federal role in mortgage markets risks undermining incentives for lenders and borrowers to make prudent decisions. If the federal government is expected to step in when economic times are bad, then lenders and borrowers do not need to consider the possibility of bad times when making decisions. The inability of current risk models to anticipate such bad times contributed to the present economic situation. Narrowly targeting federal interventions and ensuring that borrowers and lenders bear a substantial share of the costs could minimize the distortion of incentives to consider extreme risks.

It is also important to recognize that although those types of policy interventions may attenuate pricing pressures and allow a more orderly correction in the housing market, no feasible policy intervention is likely to completely stabilize house prices and mortgage markets. The main reason is that the extraordinary size of the housing market (see Table 3.1) and the magnitude of the problem would require a massive increase in the federal commitment to housing.

Large-scale federal intervention in housing markets could lead to a less efficient allocation of capital in the future. Increasing federal credit subsidies for housing would drive loan capital toward housing and away from investments that are more productive (see Box 1.1).

Table 3.1. Measures of the Size of the Housing Market

	2006	2007[a]
Annual Housing Sales (Trillions of dollars)	1.9	1.4
Housing Sales as a Share of Owner-Occupied Housing (Percent)	9	7
Total Housing Wealth (Trillions of dollars)	19.5	20.2

Source: Congressional Budget Office based on data from the Bureau of the Census, the National Association of Realtors, and the Board of Governors of the Federal Reserve System.

Note: This table compares the state of the housing market in 2006, before the credit crisis began, with the state of the market in the second half of 2007, after the crisis had taken hold.

[a]Data are from July through December.

Recent Activity by the Federal Government and Government-Sponsored Enterprises

A number of federal institutions and government-sponsored enterprises have already increased their participation in housing finance or been given more flexibility to do so.

Federal Reserve. The Federal Reserve has already started to take on some mortgage risk. On March 11, the Federal Reserve announced that it had created a new program, the Term Securities Lending Facility (TSLF), which will make loans to the 20 banks and securities firms that trade directly with the central bank. In the current situation, the Federal Reserve has found that it cannot simply provide liquidity to the overnight interbank market and expect it to flow smoothly into other parts of the financial markets. In the TSLF, the Federal Reserve offers to lend up to $200 billion of Treasury securities for 28-day terms against collateral including privately issued mortgage-backed securities [20]. The Federal Reserve has also extended through the Federal Reserve Bank of New York a loan of $29 billion to J.P. Morgan, backed by $30 billion worth of Bear Stearns' less liquid assets, in order to facilitate the acquisition of Bear Stearns by J.P. Morgan [21].

Fannie Mae and Freddie Mac. These two large federally regulated participants in the mortgage markets have recently been given more flexibility to assume additional mortgage risk. The institutions buy up pools of conforming mortgages and securitize and sell them to the secondary mortgage markets. They also hold both conforming and nonconforming mortgages as part of their portfolios. Although federal regulations restrict conforming mortgages to a certain size and creditworthiness, the size limit was recently increased from $417,000 to 125 percent of the median house price in each region (an amount up to $729,750). In addition to that temporary increase, regulators in mid-March reduced the capital reserves that the two institutions have to hold against their own portfolios of loans. According to OFHEO, that reduction is expected to provide up to $200 billion of liquidity to the MBS market.

Although a larger role for those government-sponsored enterprises helps borrowers, much of the additional underlying risk is implicitly shifted to taxpayers. Markets have taken note of the precarious financial position of Fannie Mae and Freddie Mac; the cost of purchasing insurance against default on their obligations has risen severalfold since June 2007 [22]. Prices in the credit-default swap market imply about a 7 percent probability of default over the next 10 years (versus about 3 percent last June) [23]. Moreover, Moody's has placed one of the key GSE credit ratings on review for possible downgrade. Nevertheless, the borrowing advantage of the GSEs over other corporations is likely to have increased since last summer, a demonstration of the value of the widely perceived implicit federal guarantee of their obligations.

Federal Home Loan Banks. Another set of GSEs, the Federal Home Loan Banks (FHLBs) have also intervened to support the banking industry and mortgage markets in response to the turmoil. The 12 Federal Home Loan Banks provide liquidity in housing finance markets by extending credit to various financial institutions. They take as collateral residential and commercial mortgage loans, MBSs, agency and government securities, small- business loans, and agricultural loans. During the second half of 2007, when the turmoil unfolded, FHLB advances to member financial institutions increased by $235 billion to a year-end level of $875 billion; loans to the 10 largest borrowers (including Citibank, Washington Mutual Bank, and Countrywide Bank) increased by $103 billion, to a level of $327 billion. In March, the Federal Housing Finance Board voted to double the FHLBs' authorized holdings of conforming Fannie Mae and Freddie Mac securities; the board believes that action could provide more than $100 billion to the MBS market.

Federal Housing Administration. The Federal Housing Administration (FHA) insures loans made by FHA- approved lenders and is the world's largest insurer of mortgages. It has a long tradition of assisting borrowers who would generally be considered candidates for today's troubled subprime and alt-A loans.

The economic stimulus package enacted in February increased the cap on the size of mortgages FHA may insure. That increase will allow the FHA to insure loans up to a maximum value of $729,750 in certain areas of the country.

To aid subprime ARM borrowers facing foreclosure, the Administration introduced FHA Secure in August 2007 and announced plans to expand the program in April. Originally, FHA Secure offered FHA-insured refinancing to borrowers with non-FHA adjustable-rate mortgages who were current on their loans up until the date of their first rate reset (if that reset occurs between June 2005 and December 2009). Through early April, only 2,500 mortgages of the 154,000 that FHA had refinanced since the creation of the FHA Secure program belonged to a borrower who had missed one or more payments on the previous mortgage. The remaining borrowers would have been eligible for FHA refinancing assistance that was available before the inception of FHA Secure. The program did little to assist borrowers who had missed a payment before their first reset; [24] could not afford to repay the outstanding balance under the new loan terms; or had insufficient equity in the property to meet FHA's maximum loan-to-value ratio of 97 percent.

The expanded FHA Secure program will broaden eligibility to subprime ARM borrowers who have missed up to three monthly mortgage payments irrespective of whether their inability to pay was associated with an interest rate reset. In addition, borrowers who have negotiated a reduction of loan principal with their current lender can qualify for FHA Secure insurance. For borrowers with no more than two missed monthly payments in the previous 12 months, the current lender will need to write the loan down to 97 percent or lower of the appraised value for the borrower to qualify for FHA insurance on the new loan. Borrowers with three missed monthly payments in the previous 12 months would be eligible if their loans had been written down to 90 percent or less of the currently appraised value. (See the discussion of this and related refinancing proposals under the heading "Facilitating Refinancings," below.)

Expanding the Role of the Federal Housing Administration

As the federal insurer of mortgages for nonprime borrowers, the FHA is an obvious candidate to implement an increase in direct credit intervention in the troubled sectors of the mortgage market. (Box 3.2 contains a discussion of the budgetary treatment of federal housing loan guarantees).

Increasing FHA's Maximum Loan-to-Value Ratio. FHA is currently limited to insuring mortgages with a loan-tovalue (LTV) ratio of at most 97 percent. That means FHA cannot insure restructured mortgages with no borrowers' equity. Allowing FHA to insure no-money-down mortgages might increase the resources flowing to that portion of the market.

Doing so would increase the risk to the FHA's portfolio—not because no-money-down mortgages would be significantly riskier than mortgages with a 97 percent loan-to-value ratio, but because moving into that portion of the market would increase the number of high LTV mortgages insured. That increased risk could be offset by charging higher premiums on the riskier loans.

Facilitating Refinancings. FHA could also be used to facilitate the refinancing of outstanding mortgages that are most likely to enter a costly foreclosure. The expanded FHA Secure program announced on April 9, 2008, is one such plan. Several more expansive proposals also have been discussed. Some proponents suggest that the federal role would be largely administrative, simply taking the actions that private parties would have taken were it not for impediments to sales and renegotiations in a distressed mortgage market. Others suggest that any intervention will have little effect on foreclosures without a serious commitment of taxpayers' funds. (The viability of such programs, like that of the private-sector solutions described in the previous section, would depend on the ability of servicers to gain the agreement of all parties, including second-mortgage holders).

Box 3.2. Credit Reform and Federal Housing Loan Guarantees

The budgetary treatment of actions that the federal government may take to influence housing or mortgage markets would depend on the nature of the action. Any proposals involving the direct purchase of mortgages or the issuance of insurance for privately held mortgages would follow the treatment specified in the Federal Credit Reform Act of 1990 (FCRA). Since enactment of FCRA, the federal budget has reflected the costs (or savings) from most government credit transactions on a present-value basis. For budgetary purposes, it would not matter if mortgage purchases or guarantees were made by an existing agency or a new agency created to deal with the current problems. Nearly all other (noncredit) transactions are recorded in the budget on a cash basis.

Under credit reform, the estimated net cost to the federal government of a direct loan or loan guarantee over the entire life of that loan is recorded as an outlay in the year that the loan is disbursed. The "subsidy" cost for a credit program in a particular year is the estimated net present value of all future cash flows associated with loans made during the year. Presentvalue calculations, known as discounting, are used to reflect the fact that the value today of $1 to be received in a future year is less than the value of $1 received now. FCRA rules require the calculation of present values by discounting expected cash flows at the interest rates on Treasury securities (the rates at which the government borrows money). The individual discounted cash flows, representing federal expenditures and receipts anticipated during each year of the expected life of the loans, are then summed to determine the total cost of the loans.

The Federal Housing Administration's (FHA's) Mutual Mortgage Insurance Fund is an example of a program subject to FCRA rules. Through the program, FHA provides a federal guarantee of mortgage loans funded through private lenders and state and local housing finance agencies. At the start of the 2008 budget year, FHA's portfolio of guarantees for mortgages on single-family homes was $322 billion, of which $98 billion (or 30 percent) was for mortgages that had been refinanced. The subsidy estimate for FHA loan guarantees is calculated on the basis of the contract terms of the loan guarantee and a projection of future loan terminations from prepayments and defaults. Contract terms for FHA loan guarantees include the fees charged to borrowers and the default-related expenses of lenders that FHA will reimburse. The effects of proposals that would adjust those terms—such as an increase in loan-to-value ratios, a change in equity sharing, or a strengthening of collection mechanisms—would be reflected in the estimated cash flows and subsidy rates.

Legislative proposals that would expand FHA's authority to take on risk would increase the subsidy cost of its programs (measured on a discounted present-value basis), unless additional fees were charged to offset that cost. In contrast, the full amount of grants to nonfederal entities, such as community-based organizations, state housing agencies, or government-sponsored enterprises (for example, Fannie Mae and Freddie Mac), would be recorded as outlays at the time of payment, even if such grants were ultimately used to refinance mortgages. Proposals that would allow states to issue taxexempt bonds would affect revenues because an increase in tax-exempt state borrowing would result in a loss of federal tax collections.

In one version of those proposals, mortgage servicers would put up for sale and restructuring a set of problem mortgages (which may be in mortgage pools); FHA- insured lenders would purchase those mortgages and then issue new mortgages with lower principal balances and payments that borrowers could afford. The expanded FHA Secure program will operate in a similar way, although loans need not be sold to facilitate the writedown of principal to a lower value. In another version, mortgage lenders (presumably through servicers) would themselves restructure the loans, including both first and second liens [25]. Instead of the liens, borrowers would have a new first mortgage and an interest-only loan, with the latter carrying an FHA guarantee.

The money to finance those restructurings could come from four sources. One is the investors in the current mortgages in recognition of the decline in the value of the home—the collateral for the mortgage. A second is the mortgage servicers and investors in terms of the additional costs they would have to bear from other routes to restructuring, such as foreclosure. The third is the federal government in the form of subsidized insurance from the FHA. Finally, another source of financing is the value of possible future increases in the price of the house. That is, some of the gain from a higher price when the house is sold could be assigned to the lender or taxpayers, as in a shared-appreciation loan. Lenders would be more willing to write down their loan in exchange for a share of future appreciation in the property. Assigning some of the future gain to taxpayers would reduce the cost of the federal subsidy.

The number of borrowers that could be assisted by such proposals would depend directly on the amount of mortgage insurance subsidy that the government provides. With moderate refinancing fees, as embodied in most recent proposals, the federal subsidy would probably amount to less than 5 percent of the new loan principal, on average. Given that scale of subsidy, CBO expects that perhaps several hundred thousand borrowers would benefit from expanded FHA-insured refinancings over the next few years. Generating higher levels of participation would require substantially deeper subsidies, which would in turn significantly increase the federal budget cost. (Under current law, any subsidy costs for FHA loan guarantees are subject to appropriation of the necessary funds. Annual appropriation acts also generally limit the dollar amount of new federal loan guarantees that FHA can enter into for a given year.)

The creation of borrowers' equity is important to such proposals. Mortgages for which the outstanding balance exceeds the value of the property are most likely to go into foreclosure because borrowers who have no equity will find few options for refinancing and will be more willing to walk away from a mortgage that they are struggling to pay. Restructurings with no federal involvement are not likely to involve any significant borrowers' equity, either. Indeed, many would leave borrowers with lower monthly payments but negative equity in the house. Unfortunately, even restructurings that create positive equity may not be a permanent solution. In a declining housing market, such equity may be evanescent, and the risk of redefault is thus likely to grow until house prices stop falling.

Distribution of Benefits. The benefits of any resources that the federal government provides to support the restructuring of mortgages (such as subsidized FHA guarantees) are likely to be shared among borrowers and lenders. While borrowers whose loans are restructured will not have to move from one home to another and will have lower mortgage payments, some might get approximately the same benefits from a lender-initiated restructuring without federal intervention. Lenders (through their servicers) have strong incentives to avoid defaults and foreclosures. Lenders will receive a windfall on those loans that they would have restructured without federal assistance. Despite that, lenders will be willing to restructure more mortgages with federal subsidies than without them.

The distribution of benefits will have an impact on the decision of borrowers and lenders to participate in the program. In a purchase and refinance program, the government would separately set the level of assistance to borrowers and lenders. Those levels would need to be carefully chosen to ensure that borrowers and lenders had enough incentive to participate. For example, the government might offer a write-down for certain types of loans, and lenders would choose to offer eligible loans for sale at that write-down. Lenders will only offer up loans where they anticipate that the terms of sale exceed the value of the best alternative for dealing with each loan. Similarly, the assistance offered to borrowers would have to be generous enough to ensure that their new loan was affordable.

In a loan restructuring program (one that does not involve loan sales), the distribution of benefits would be decided by negotiation between borrowers and lenders, subject to any constraints imposed by the program's regulations. If regulations were to mandate, as a condition of federal support, a restructuring package that was too generous to borrowers, lenders might offer few mortgages for restructuring. If the restructuring package was not generous enough to borrowers, lenders might fear that the restructuring would not be effective at preventing further defaults. Moreover, borrowers might decide to walk away rather than accept the package. And even if regulation simply mandated that lenders use a single restructuring package—for example, writing down all loans by the same percentage below market and setting mortgage payments on the basis of the same interest rate—fewer loans might be restructured than if the lender could tailor the package to the borrower's credit and the lender's expectations of future price declines in the local housing market.

Price of a Loan. The price offered to holders of the existing mortgage (or mortgages) could be established by either a fixed write-down of the appraised value of the property or via an auction in which federally approved bidders would pay for pools of mortgage loans put up for sale by current servicers. Proponents of an auction argue that it could help reignite the secondary market for non-prime loans and enable a more efficient process of refinancing loans in bulk. The benefits of bulk refinancing might not materialize, however, as servicers would still need to decide on a case-by-case basis whether to offer loans into the program, and borrowers would still need to participate in the drafting of new loans.

Loan servicers will only sell a mortgage if they perceive that the price offered exceeds the price a private buyer might pay for it, the value of renegotiating the loan privately with the borrower, and the net proceeds from foreclosure. Servicers will be willing to take a substantial discount on the amount owed on loans for which foreclosure is the best alternative because of the high costs of foreclosure. One concern for taxpayers in a program that has a fixed write-down of the appraisal value is that it would give existing mortgage holders incentive to offer mortgages that were only worth less than that value. That adverse selection would impose higher costs on taxpayers for a given volume of guarantees.

Eligibility of Borrowers. The program would need to maintain a delicate balance between assisting borrowers who are unable to refinance or repay their current loans and excluding those borrowers who can. Screening borrowers using established affordability criteria would help, but borrowers would have incentives to understate their ability to pay. To discourage borrowers who do not need government assistance, the terms of the refinanced loan must be made sufficiently unattractive to make that loan desirable only to those with a true inability to pay. Such measures could include restricting program participants from taking second mortgages on the property, or forcing borrowers to share any equity gains in their loans with taxpayers.

Additional restrictions and provisions could be applied to refinanced loans to minimize the cost to taxpayers. FHA could compel borrowers to provide adequate documentation to certify that they can afford their new loans. Federal assistance might also be limited to owner-occupied principal residences. However, because verifying a claim of principal residence is difficult, many investors may be able to take advantage of such programs unless the process of verification is more stringent than the current underwriting process [26].

Many loan restructurings will end in default. To help reduce the cost of those defaults to the federal government, the program could specify that borrowers who subsequently default be subjected to stronger collection mechanisms, such as those in the Treasury Offset program. In the Treasury Offset program, an individual's federal transfer payments—such as Social Security payments and federal income tax refunds—can be used to pay down delinquent federal loans or guarantees. Such an approach would be a more severe collection program than borrowers would typically face from private lenders: In some states, lenders have no legal recourse to assets or income beyond the value of the property; and even where recourse is legally available, lenders often do not pursue it for subprime borrowers, who are not expected to have significant assets beyond the mortgage collateral.

Further Expanding the Role of Fannie Mae and Freddie Mac

The Congress could also consider mandating that Fannie Mae and Freddie Mac play a larger role in supporting the financing of subprime mortgages [27].

The GSEs could be required to securitize subprime loans—a requirement that would offer the GSEs the opportunity to make money from guarantee fees, which would reflect the risk of those securities—or to hold more subprime or alt-A mortgages in their portfolios. Various legislative proposals also have been made to have the GSEs contribute to affordable housing funds, which would support lower-income subprime borrowers.

Minimizing the risk to taxpayers of such an increase in the GSEs' portfolios would require an increase in the GSEs' capital. Both housing GSEs have experienced recent governance, financial, and accounting control problems as well as large losses on their subprime mortgage holdings. Taxpayers have been protected from having those losses shifted to them, however, by the GSEs' capital. Even though financial markets are distressed, the GSEs are likely to be able to raise new funds for subprime mortgage lending. With the support of an implicit federal guarantee of their debt and other liabilities, Fannie Mae and Freddie Mac have privileged access to funds in the capital markets. During times of financial turmoil and uncertainty, when there is often a "flight to quality" by investors, the securities issued by those entities tend to be favored investments.

Working through the GSEs, however, would give the government less control over the use of taxpayers' money. The federal government could not dictate the terms of assistance as readily as it could if it expanded one of the federal agencies (such as FHA), because of the GSEs' for- profit charter [28]. Thus, there is a significant possibility that taxpayers might take on additional risk through the

GSEs' expansion, but not all the value of that additional risk-bearing would go to the desired borrowers.

Expanding the Role of Federal Home Loan Banks

A less direct way to support the mortgage markets would be to follow the lead of the Federal Reserve by increasing the provision of liquidity to banks using the Federal Home Loan Banks as a conduit. The additional liquidity could be made conditional on banks' meeting specified refinancing, forbearance, or loan-modification objectives. That approach would put the onus on banks to devise specific strategies for resolving problems in the mortgage market. It would also make use of the banks' capital cushions, thus reducing the risk to taxpayers.

To do that, the FHLBs would need either more capital or reduced capital requirements. As with Fannie Mae and Freddie Mac, reducing capital requirements would increase the risk that taxpayers could be embroiled in a costly bailout if one or more of the banks failed.

Increasing Federal Assistance to Community-Based Organizations

Another approach would increase federal assistance to community-based organizations, such as community development corporations and community development financial institutions that provide services, counseling, and foreclosure protection to households [29]. Among other things, counseling may help steer borrowers to prime markets and away from subprime markets and may also be used to make delinquent borrowers aware of alternatives to foreclosure. In 2008, the Congress appropriated $50 million for the Department of Housing and Urban Development's Housing Counseling Assistance Program. The program provides counseling services to eligible homeowners and tenants, including home purchase, financial management, and rental counseling. (The Home Ownership and Equity Protection Act of 1994 has no provisions requiring counseling; however, some states require lenders to notify borrowers of counseling opportunities.)

In addition, the Congress provided $180 million to the Neighborhood Reinvestment Corporation for mortgage mitigation activities [30]. A bill passed by the House would require lenders to alert delinquent borrowers to counseling opportunities, some of which could be provided by housing advocacy groups [31].

Creating a New Agency

Instead of using existing agencies, the government could create a new agency, either to buy subprime mortgages or to make loans directly to borrowers.

Although an existing agency could be given the same responsibilities as a new agency, a new limited-purpose agency would have a focused charter and could be set up to "sunset" (expire) after a reasonable amount of time. By contrast, expanding the scope of an existing agency's mission to include providing subsidies would force the new program to compete for resources and management time with the agency's other responsibilities. Moreover, the new responsibility could become regarded as part of the permanent mission of the agency, thus making it harder to end when the urgent need was over.

Setting up a new agency, however, is usually complicated and time-consuming. A recent example is provided by the Resolution Trust Corporation (RTC), which was created to address the thrift crisis of the 1980s. Although it was a new, independent agency, the RTC was staffed by employees from other federal agencies, mainly the Federal Deposit Insurance Corporation. During the six years it operated, the RTC resolved 747 failed thrifts with $394 billion of assets [32]. In its first 5 months, the RTC took over 318 failed thrifts but resolved only 37 of them. The situation for the RTC improved in the subsequent 12 months, and the RTC was able to resolve 315 institu tions. The RTC's experience highlights two challenges with setting up a new agency. Policymakers faced significant difficulties in providing additional funding for the RTC after its initial $50 billion in funding proved insufficient. The agency also faced persistent criticism—some founded, some unfounded—about its operations and the complex management structure of the corporation and its oversight board [33]. Moreover, the RTC was in a situation that differs significantly from the current one: It was created to accelerate the breakup of the thrifts because, as long as they continued to operate, they were taking on ever-riskier investments [34].

Buying Subprime Mortgages. A new agency could purchase problematic loans at steep discounts. That approach was used by the Home Owners' Loan Corporation, when it exchanged bonds for defaulted mortgages with lenders and investors at a discount and adjusted the loan terms to help borrowers during the Depression.

Proponents believe that such a program could put a floor on the prices of subprime mortgages and allow market participants to price the assets of financial institutions. The agency would aim to sell the mortgages at higher prices when financial markets were better able to price them and were more amenable to undertaking the risk. That would still leave the agency exposed to the risk of a delayed recovery in the housing market, which could keep mortgage prices depressed for many years and, hence, offer a poor return on investment to taxpayers.

Making Direct Loans to Borrowers. Instead of buying mortgages, a new agency could make loans directly to borrowers at affordable rates [35]. Borrowers would use the proceeds from the more affordable loans to prepay a fraction of their outstanding mortgage (or mortgages, if theyhad a second lien). That approach could get around the difficulty of obtaining agreement for mortgage restructuring from second-mortgage holders and MBS investors, since it would go through the procedures for prepayment established under the terms of their original mortgage contracts, including any penalties for early repayment [36].

The number of borrowers with troubled mortgages who would be willing to take a federal loan would depend on the terms offered. Borrowers would have to be able to afford to make their combined monthly payment on the new loan and the remaining portion of the old loan. For the payment to be affordable for borrowers, the federal loan may need to offer below-market interest rates and a long term to maturity. In addition, the loan would need to replace a large enough portion of the original unaffordable mortgage.

Loans made at below-market terms to borrowers with negative equity in their property would be costly to taxpayers. The combination of negative equity and a history of missed payments on the original mortgage suggests that the probability of default on a direct loan would be high. A federal loan would be likely to have lower claim on the property than the borrower's preexisting loans. The government could strengthen the enforceability of the direct loan by making it nondischargeable in bankruptcy and subject to stronger collection mechanisms than privately issued loans. If the federal loan and original loans were adjustable-rate mortgages, affordability prob lems could resurface if short-term interest rates increased from their present historically low levels.

Like a purchase and refinance program, a direct lending program would face a similar challenge in restricting eligibility to borrowers who could not afford their existing mortgage but could afford their new mortgage. If the new loans carried interest rate terms that were significantly below those on prime mortgages, then borrowers of all types would be clamoring to participate.

Providing Mortgage Assistance. Through States Federal assistance to borrowers might also be channeled through states. Options for financing such assistance include expanding authority for tax-exempt bonds or providing direct grants to states. Less directly, federal grants to states might finance programs to help borrowers navigate through the process of restructuring their loans.

Currently, state-based housing agencies are eligible to issue tax-exempt bonds to finance new mortgages for first-time homebuyers. Tax-exempt debt allows states to finance at interest rates that are significantly lower than the rate on comparable taxable debt, the benefits of which can be passed on to borrowers. Expanding states' borrowing authority to refinance mortgages, however, would reduce federal income tax receipts.

Comparatively, tax-exempt financing is a less cost- effective means of transferring resources from the federal government to state and local governments. Because of the progressive structure of the federal income tax, the revenue loss to the federal government from those tax- exempt bonds exceeds the debt-service savings to states and localities. More direct means of transferring resources, such as grants, deliver more aid at a smaller cost to the federal government.

References

Section 1

[1] The percentage of homes with subprime ARMs entering foreclosure was a record 5.3 percent in the fourth quarter of 2007, up from 2.7 percent at the end of 2006 and 1.6 percent at the end of 2005. At the end of 2007, more than 13 percent of subprime ARMs were in the process of foreclosure

[2] CDOs repackage assets such as mortgage bonds, buyout loans, and other debt (including other CDOs) into new securities

Section 2

[1] Measures of house prices differ substantially in their coverage and how they handle changes in quality. OFHEO's index covers all areas of the country and has a relatively sophisticated adjustment for quality—which is a big issue in house prices—but it is restricted to houses with conforming mortgages (those eligible for purchase by Fannie Mae and Freddie Mac, two government- sponsored enterprises). The S&P/Case-Shiller indexes use the same adjustment for quality but cover fewer geographic areas. However, they include all homes in a covered area, whatever the type of mortgage. The Radar Logic composite index covers just 25 metropolitan housing markets and is not intended to represent the national market. It reflects all

transactions, including sales of condominiums, and is updated daily. Its only quality adjustment, however, is for the size of the residence.

[2] Futures contracts based on that index trade on the Chicago Mercantile Exchange. Trading in those contracts is akin to taking a position on what the value of the index will be in the future, say 12 months ahead. If, after that time, the value of the index is above the futures price the buyer paid, the seller pays the buyer the difference between the index and the futures price. However, if the value of the index is below the futures price, the buyer pays the seller the difference. Such contracts may be useful as a hedge against the real estate market. Futures prices may not be a reliable guide to expectations, though, particularly for longer periods. Futures contracts of this kind do not trade frequently or in large numbers and therefore may not represent a consensus of investors.

The S&P/Case-Shiller 10-City Composite Home Price Index tracks changes in the value of residential real estate in 10 metropolitan regions. No futures markets are associated with the S&P/ Case-Shiller 20-city or national price indexes.

[3] A loan is delinquent when a borrower misses a contractual payment. The numbers cited in the text refer to loans that are at least 30 days overdue. Foreclosure is a legal proceeding to terminate a borrower's interest in a property, instituted by the lender either to gain title or to force a sale to satisfy the unpaid debt secured by the property.

[4] On average, mortgages actually last only about seven years because people sell or refinance. Thus, the appropriate comparison is to a seven-year Treasury note rather than to an investment with a longer term to maturity.

[5] Libor, the London Interbank Offered Rate, is the rate at which banks lend to each other for short terms

[6] ABX.HE indexes are calculated by the Markit Group Limited. ABX index values are based on the up-front premiums for credit default swaps on underlying subprime MBSs. The values of ABX indexes move inversely with the cost of ensuring that the holder of an MBS will receive all principal and interest payments.

[7] Mortgage-backed securities are repackaged in tranches, or securities of different seniority, in payment from the MBSs. An MBS with higher seniority, such as the most senior of the AAA-rated tranches, is entitled to payments before those in tranches with lower seniority, such as a less senior AAA tranche or any lower- rated tranche. In other words, a less senior tranche realizes a loss on an MBS before a more senior tranche.

[8] Usually it is the most junior tranche of a given credit rating that is selected for the index. There are no indexes for MBSs based on subprime securities originated in the second half of 2007 because almost no such mortgages were originated

[9] See Congressional Budget Office, *The Budget and Economic Outlook: Fiscal Years 2008 to 2018* (January 2008), Chapter 2, for a fuller discussion of recent problems in financial markets.

[10] The spread between those two rates is an indicator of credit risk. The three-month Libor provides funding among participants who may not have access to Federal Reserve liquidity facilities. Federal funds, in contrast, are overnight and shorter-term funding between banks with access to the Federal Reserve discount window. They typically have higher collateral standards than for Libor.

[11] The $500 billion figure is calculated by CBO from estimates in David Greenlaw and others, "Leveraged Losses: Lessons from the Mortgage Market Meltdown" (U.S. Monetary Policy Forum Conference Draft, February 2008). That figure represents 4.6 percent of the value of outstanding mortgages. The $600 billion figure was calculated on the basis of the statement of Mark Zandi, Moody's Economy.com, "The Looming Foreclosure Crisis: How to Help Families Save Their Homes," before the Senate Committee on the Judiciary (December 5, 2007), in which the author estimated 2.8 million mortgages, or over 5 percent, would enter foreclosure through 2009.

[12] Bloomberg LLC, Asset write-downs and credit losses table, April 1, 2008.

[13] Public Law 110-185; 122 Stat. 613.

[14] The law's provisions will subtract about 0.4 percentage points from growth of real GDP in 2009, CBO estimates, as most of the stimulus is removed.

[15] Primary dealers are banks or securities broker-dealers who may trade directly with the Federal Reserve System.

[16] The discount rate is the rate paid by banks borrowing from the Federal Reserve. The Federal Reserve sets a target rate for the federal funds, the rate banks charge each other for overnight loans. The Board of Governors of the Federal Reserve System can cut discount rates only when it has a request to do so from a Federal Reserve Bank. By March 20, all banks had requested cuts to a new spread of 25 basis points over the target for the federal funds rate. (A basis point is one-hundredth of a percentage point.)

Section 3

[1] Six of the largest mortgage servicers, accounting for 50 percent of the mortgage-servicing market, announced on February 12 a plan called Project Lifeline, which specifies the conditions under which a mortgage borrower who is 90 days or more delinquent may be allowed an extra 30 days to work out a loan modification

[2] Hope Now, an alliance of various participants in mortgage markets, reports that since July 2007, it has helped more than 1 million borrowers, about 640,000 of whom have subprime credit ratings. Loans were modified for about 25 percent of the borrowers assisted by Hope Now.

[3] In some cases, borrowers took out two mortgages: a first mortgage (or lien) at 80 percent of the value of the home and a second mortgage for as much as the remaining 20 percent of the home's value. The second mortgage financed some or all of the down- payment and allowed borrowers to avoid paying mortgage insurance on the first lien.

[4] A short sale is a sale at a price that is lower than the total value of the mortgages on the house

[5] Priority among lien holders is determined by state property law. A minority (but growing) view among the states is that a previously subordinate lien will be resubordinated as a matter of law unless the new loan modifies the obligations of the borrower in a way that is materially prejudicial to the holders of the junior liens. Examples of modifications that may be prejudicial include increasing the principal of the first lien or increasing the interest rate. See Restatement (Third) of Property: Mortgages §7.6 (1997); *Bank of America v. Prestance Corp.*, 160 P.3d 17, 21 (Wash. 2007); and Grant S. Nelson and Dale A. Whitman, "Adopting Restatement Mortgage Subrogation Principles: Saving Billions of Dollars for Refinancing Homeowners," *Brigham Young University Law Review* (2006), p. 305. The majority view is that a previously subordinate lien will not be resubordinated if the refinancing lender has actual knowledge of the other liens. The remaining states would withhold resubordination if the refinancing lender has even constructive knowledge of the other liens or if the refinancing lender is a volunteer to the transaction.

[6] The transaction costs associated with obtaining such agreement are avoided in states where second liens are automatically resubordinate.

[7] The ASF Framework is the American Securitization Forum's "Statement of Principles, Recommendations, and Guidelines for a Streamlined Foreclosure and Loss Avoidance Framework for Securitized Subprime Adjustable Rate

Mortgage Loans." See Rev. Proc. 2007-72, 2007-52 I.R.B. 1257; SEC Office of Chief Accountant letter, January 8, 2008, available at www.sec.gov/info/ accountants/staffletters/hanish010808.pdf. The ASF Framework applies to first-lien subprime residential adjustable-rate mortgage loans that have an initial fixed-rate period of 36 months or less (including "2/28s" and "3/27s"); were originated between January 1, 2005, and July 31, 2007; are included in securitized pools; and have an initial interest rate that resets between January 1, 2008, and July 31, 2010. The framework provides a fast-track procedure for modifying loans and details the criteria for determining which loans are eligible for the procedure. In a fast-track modification, the interest rate on the affected loan will be kept at the existing rate, generally for five years after the date on which the rate would have reset had the modification not occurred.

[8] Most of the pooling and servicing agreements were executed before the IRS and the Chief Accountant of the Securities and Exchange Commission reached their decisions regarding the ASF Framework. Consequently, some of those agreements may contain provisions that are more restrictive than what could now be permitted under the framework.

[9] See H.R. 5579, the Emergency Mortgage Loan Modification Act of 2008, and the amendments intended to be proposed by Senator Specter (No. 4408) and by Senator Reid for Senator Clinton (No. 4492) to H.R. 3221, the New Direction for Energy Independence, National Security, and Consumer Protection Act.

[10] Until recently, borrowers had faced taxes based on the loss forced upon the mortgage holder when the lender took back ownership of the home. That served as a disincentive to walk away. However, the Congress temporarily excluded from taxation the gains on certain mortgage debt forgiven on principal residences and extended the deduction for premiums paid on private mortgage insurance in the Mortgage Forgiveness Debt Relief Act of 2007 (Public Law 110-142; 121 Stat. 1803.

[11] That agreement was arranged by the Treasury Department and the Department of Housing and Urban Development, with lenders, servicers, mortgage counselors, and investors.

[12] In "The Potential Effect of Rate Freezes on S&P-Rated U.S. First- Lien Subprime RMBS" (December 14, 2007), Standard & Poor's estimated that about 20 percent of the 1.2 million subprime adjustable-rate first mortgages would be eligible for fast-track modification. In March, it was reported that the Clayton Group expected about 50,000 of those loans eventually to be modified under terms of the voluntary agreement.

In "The Mixed Impact of Falling Rates on U.S. Alt-A and Subprime Borrowers," Standard & Poor's (March 26, 2008), the authors found that because of the sharp drop in the Libor, subprime borrowers facing an interest rate reset will on average pay a rate just 1 percentage point higher than their initial "teaser" rate. They also found that the lower Libor had "virtually eliminated Alt-A payment shock."

[13] Kristopher Gerardi, Adam Shapiro, and Paul Willen, "Subprime Outcomes: Risky Mortgages, Homeownership Experiences, and Foreclosures" (Federal Reserve Bank of Boston Working Paper, December 2007)

[14] Proposals for shared-appreciation loans must ensure that the obligations would be legal, valid, and binding and receive the intended priority in foreclosure and bankruptcy proceedings.

[15] Borrowers would face some consequences by defaulting: a lower credit rating and, in some states, an attempt by lenders to gain title to some of their other assets (although recovery of that type has been rare so far).

[16] Gerardi, Shapiro, and Willen, "Subprime Outcomes." Borrowers have what essentially amounts to a put option—if the value of the house falls below the amount owed, they may be better off abandoning the house. See, for example, Ronel Elul, "Residential Mortgage Default," *Business Review* (Federal Reserve Bank of Philadelphia, 2006); and Michael LaCour-Little, "Equity Dilution: An Alternative Perspective on Mortgage Default," *Real Estate Economics* (September 2004).

[17] 11 U.S.C. §1322(b)(2). Furthermore, the Supreme Court held that even when the value of the debt exceeds the value of the property—a partially secured debt—courts may not modify that debt. See *Nobleman v. Am. Savings Bank*, 508 U.S. 324 (1993). Conversely, when a second (or third) mortgage is wholly unsecured because the value of the property is insufficient to satisfy the first mortgage, such subordinated debt may be discharged; *Tanner v. FirstPlus Fin. Inc.* (*In re Tanner*), 217 F. 3d 1357 (11th Cir. 2000) announced what has become the dominant view among the circuit courts of appeals. Hence, the claims of partially secured creditors are protected by bankruptcy law, but the claims of unsecured creditors are not.

[18] See Adam J. Levitin and Joshua Goodman, *The Effect of Bankruptcy Strip-Down on Mortgage Markets,* Business Economics and Regulatory Policy Working Paper No. 1087816 (Georgetown University Law Center, February 6, 2008).

[19] Congressional Budget Office, cost estimate for H.R. 3609, the Emergency Home Ownership and Mortgage Equity Protection Act of 2007, as ordered

reported by the House Committee on the Judiciary on December 12, 2007 (February 5, 2008).

[20] Details of the program are available at the Federal Reserve's Web site, www.federalreserve.gov/monetarypolicy/tslf.htm.

[21] A press release states that the Federal Reserve Bank of New York "will take, through a limited liability company formed for this purpose, control of a portfolio of assets valued at $30 billion as of March 14, 2008. The assets will be pledged as security for $29 billion in term financing from the New York Fed at its primary credit rate. JPMorgan Chase will bear the first $1 billion of any losses associated with the portfolio and any realized gains will accrue to the New York Fed. BlackRock Financial Management, Inc. will manage the portfolio under guidelines established by the New York Fed designed to minimize disruption to financial markets and maximize recovery value." See the Federal Reserve Bank of New York's "Statement on Financing Arrangement of JPMorgan Chase's Acquisition of Bear Stearns," available at www.newyork fed.org/newsevents/news/markets/2008/rp080324.html.

[22] The cost of $10 million of protection has climbed from about $8,000 in June to about $45,000 as of early April.

[23] A credit default swap is a contractual arrangement in which the buyer pays a premium at periodic intervals in exchange for a contingent payment in the event of the default of some third party. The size of the premium paid relative to the contingent payment generally increases with the likelihood of default.

[24] For adjustable-rate subprime mortgages made in 2006, about 10 percent had defaulted in the first 12 months. See Board of Governors of the Federal Reserve System, *Monetary Report to the Congress* (February 2008).

[25] Mark M. Zandi, Richard Jaffee, and Daniel Melser, *Home App reciation Mortgage Plan,* Moody's Economy.com, March 2008.

[26] Over the past several years, many mortgages for owner-occupied property were actually obtained by investors

[27] Lawrence Summers, "This Is Where Fannie and Freddie Step In," *Financial Times,* August 26, 2007; and statement of Alex Pollock, resident fellow, American Enterprise Institute, "Legislative and Regulatory Options Regarding Mortgage Foreclosures," before the House Committee on Financial Services (September 20, 2007).

[28] See Douglas W. Elmendorf, "What Should Be Done to Help Households Facing Foreclosure?" (Brookings Institution, November 2007), available at www.brookings.edu/opinions/ 2007/1 1_mortgages_elmendorf.aspx.

[29] Edward M. Gramlich, *Subp rime Mortgages: America's Latest Boom and Bust* (Washington, D.C.: Urban Institute Press, 2007).

[30] Consolidated Appropriations Act of 2008 (Public Law 110-161; 121 Stat. 1844).

[31] H.R. 1852, *Expanding American Homeownership Act of 2007.*

[32] Resolving the 747 failed thrifts cost the RTC $83 billion, financed by $76 billion from the U.S. Treasury and $7 billion from the private sector. See Timothy Curry and Lynn Shibut, "The Cost of the Saving and Loan Crisis: Truth and Consequences," *FDIC Banking Review,* vol. 13, no. 2 (2000).

[33] See Lee Davison, "The Resolution Trust Corporation and Congress, 1989–1993 (Part I and II)," *FDIC Banking Review,* vol. 18, nos. 1 and 2 (2006).

[34] Note, however, that deposit insurance transactions are reflected in the budget on a cash basis, unlike the costs of federal loans and loan guarantees, which are recorded on a present-value basis.

[35] Martin Feldstein, "How to Stop the Mortgage Crisis," *The Wall Street Journal,* March 7, 2008.

[36] As of February 2008, about 70 percent of subprime loans and about 40 percent of alt-A loans featured prepayment penalties if the loan was prepaid within an initial period of generally two to three years, according to tabulations made by researchers at the New York Federal Reserve Bank from a sample of loans in First American Loan Performance's database.

In: Financial Crisis in America ISBN 978-1-60692-191-3
Editor: Raymond T. Ovanhouser, pp. 47-75

Chapter 2

FINANCIAL CRISIS? THE LIQUIDITY CRUNCH OF AUGUST 2007*

Darryl E. Getter, Mark Jickling, Marc Labonte and Edward V. Murphy

ABSTRACT

Firms are said to be liquid when they are able to meet current obligations or short-term demand for funds. A firm is said to be solvent but illiquid when its assets exceed its liabilities but it is unable to liquidate assets rapidly enough to meet current obligations. Markets are said to be liquid when a large volume of financial securities can be traded without price distortions because there is a ready and willing supply of buyers and sellers. Liquid markets are a sign of normalcy.

In August 2007, liquidity abruptly dried up for many firms and securities markets. Suddenly some firms were able to borrow and investors were able to sell certain securities only at prohibitive rates and prices, if at all. The liquidity crunch was most extreme for firms and securities with links to subprime mortgages, but it also spread rapidly into seemingly unrelated areas. The stock market experienced unusual volatility and investors rushed to buy the safest of all investments, U.S. Treasury securities. On August 31, Federal Reserve Chairman Ben Bernanke noted that "[a]lthough this episode appears to have been triggered largely by heightened concerns about

* Excerpted from CRS Report RL34182, dated September 21, 2007.

subprime mortgages, global financial losses have far exceeded even the most pessimistic projections of credit losses on those loans."

The spread of disruptions from housing into other debt markets is an example of financial contagion, or systemic risk. Contagion spread among non-bank institutions: mortgage lenders, hedge funds, and issuers of various types of securities, including commercial paper, asset-backed securities, structured products, and debt supporting leveraged buyouts and takeovers. As fear of risk has increased, these institutions saw sources of credit vanish and struggled to meet existing financing commitments, to post additional collateral, and to cope with portfolio losses. Some financial institutions, primarily mortgage lenders and hedge funds, have been unable to resolve liquidity problems and have closed. In the months ahead, there may be more failures.

Central banks, including the Federal Reserve, have responded by providing liquidity — injecting cash into the banking system and lowering interest rates — in order to prevent financial disruptions from slowing real economic growth. While financial "paper losses" have no direct effect on output or employment, there are channels through which changes in financial conditions may be transmitted to the real economy: for example, tight credit and equity markets restrain business investment in plant and equipment.

In the wake of the liquidity crunch, policymakers may consider several areas for reform. Could regulation have prevented current problems in the mortgage market? Should credit rating agencies, like Moody's and Standard and Poor's, be subject to more oversight by the Securities and Exchange Commission? Should the non-bank institutions that have been central to this episode be subject to greater regulatory supervision or information disclosure requirements? This chapter analyzes the causes, progress, and broad policy issues raised by recent liquidity problems, but does not address proposals to alleviate distress in the housing sector.

INTRODUCTION

Financial markets suffered significant disruption in August 2007. Certain financial instruments, especially mortgage-backed collateralized debt obligations (CDOs), became illiquid, that is, they became difficult to sell at any price. Liquidity problems then spread across other credit markets as investors feared that losses linked to housing securities might affect a broad range of market participants. There was a "flight to quality" as investors shifted funds into the least risky securities, such as U.S. Treasury securities. As a result, many types of corporate and financial borrowers — even some with few or no links to mortgage markets — had trouble obtaining credit, whether to fund new projects or transactions, or to refinance existing debt. The stock market experienced unusual volatility, although the Dow Jones Industrial Average actually gained 156 points during August.

The financial volatility observed in August is particularly significant because it illustrates how stress in one financial market — in this case, housing — may spread to other markets, causing losses to investors and intermediaries not directly involved in the market where the trouble originated. These events raise questions about the ability of policymakers to respond to financial crises since an increasing share of credit market activity now occurs outside the banking system, in unregulated institutions such as nonbank mortgage lenders and hedge funds.

This chapter describes the preceding events that instigated the August 2007 liquidity crunch, followed by the major events that occurred during the crunch. It then analyzes the structure of financial markets today to identify underlying causes for the crunch. It ends by analyzing policy issues raised by the liquidity crunch relating to macroeconomic stabilization policy and financial regulation.

How We Got Here

The Housing Boom and Bust

House prices in some regions grew rapidly after interest rates declined in 2001. Adjusting for inflation, real U.S. house prices rose 34% during 2000-2005 (they rose 51% if not adjusted), which is more than double any five-year rate in the past 30 years. Specific regions experienced even faster appreciation; in 2004 alone, housing in Miami, Los Angeles, and West Palm Beach appreciated more than 20% and Las Vegas appreciated 35%. Figure 1 shows that the rate of house price appreciation, year over year, reached 13% in 2006, and then plunged to 3% by mid-2007. There are three important points to make about this figure. First, as of mid-2007, average prices of single family homes were not yet falling, according to the Office of Federal Housing Oversight's home price index (although prices were already falling according to some other data sources). Many housing analysts believe that prices in this data set may be lagging actual prices, however. Second, national averages mask regional differences. Prices in certain areas are still appreciating relatively rapidly, whereas other areas are currently declining. Third, types of housing not covered by this data series, such as condominiums, may have experienced a very different pattern of appreciation.

In rapidly appreciating regions, many borrowers refinanced their mortgages quickly, both because they could tap this new equity for other purposes and because the increased equity could improve their credit profile and allow them to borrow on better terms.

Source: Office of Federal Housing Enterprise Oversight.

Notes: The figure is based on a repeat sales index of single family homes with conventional loans. It measures the nominal appreciation in price of a given house from the first time it was sold to the second time it was sold.

Figure 1. Appreciation of House Prices, 1996-2007.

As a result, mortgage products designed to be refinanced after a short period of time, such as so-called 2/28s, "interest only" adjustable rate mortgages (ARMs), ARMs with "teaser rates," and option ARMs, [1] became increasingly popular in hot regional markets. Subprime borrowers (i.e., borrowers with weak credit profiles) were attracted to alternative mortgages to take advantage of growing equity's effect on their credit profile. Investors were attracted to alternative mortgages because they allowed larger purchases with less money down, often with little documentation (so-called low-doc or Alt-A mortgages) [2]. As long as house prices continued to rise, borrowers in hot markets easily refinanced their loans or sold their homes at a profit, and delinquency rates remained low. Noting low delinquency rates, more loans with lower underwriting standards began to be made. This can be seen in the rapid growth of the subprime mortgage market, shown in Figure 2.

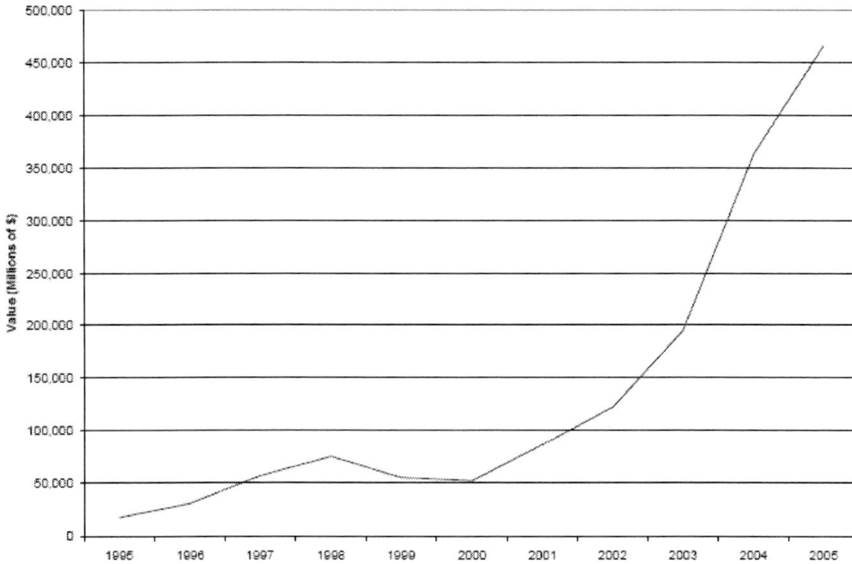

Source: Inside Mortgage Finance, *2007 Mortgage Market Statistical Annual*, vol 1., p. 3.

Figure 2. Subprime Mortgage-Backed Securities.

In 2005, $507.9 billion in subprime mortgage loans were pooled and sold as mortgage- backed securities (MBS), compared with $18.5 billion in 1995 [3].

When interest rates began rising and house price appreciation slowed, many borrowers in the subprime market found it impossible to refinance on favorable terms and were unable to maintain their mortgage payments when their loans reset. There is now evidence that many borrowers in the Alt-A market are having similar problems. At the same time, house sales fell rapidly, making it more difficult to quickly exit a troubled mortgage by selling. Traditionally, delinquency and default rates have been closely tied to local economic conditions, but these rates are rising today even in some areas that have relatively low unemployment and strong local economies as well. In several formerly hot markets, prices began to fall even though local unemployment remained low. For example, several Florida cities were among the weakest housing markets even though Florida's unemployment rate of 3.9% remained below the U.S. average of 4.6% in July 2007.

Furthermore, surveys of mortgages originated in 2005 suggest that defaults and foreclosures will rise even higher in late 2007 and the first half of 2008. As a result, potential buyers of MBS now demand greater detail about the composition of their securities in an effort to determine their exposure to poorly underwritten loans. In the past, buyers might rely on the rating agencies to label the risk-level of a loan pool, but events have shown that the ratings agencies underestimated the risk — there have been several examples of MBS downgraded from the least-risky AAA rating to CCC (near-default) overnight [4]. Troubles in housing markets thus caused uncertainty in financial markets and reduced the liquidity of loans and securities backed by loans.

Was the Boom a Bubble? In the aftermath of the housing boom, the question that economists are heatedly debating is how much of the increase in housing prices was due to economic fundamentals, and how much was due to a bubble — a rise in price due to "irrational exuberance" about future price appreciation, in the famous words of Alan Greenspan. A bubble would be consistent with many borrowers taking on mortgages that they could not really afford in the belief that they could borrow against the property when prices rose or "flip" the property by quickly selling it at a profit after prices rise. These borrowers may find their position untenable now that prices in local markets are instead flat or falling and sales have slowed [5]. There were also reasons for house prices to rise based on market "fundamentals," however, such as rising incomes and falling mortgage rates.

As discussed above, mortgage rates during the housing boom were low by historical standards, but that does not necessarily imply that they would stay low. This raises two questions about housing market behavior. First, why did borrowers increasingly use ARMs rather than locking in a relatively low fixed rate, which would have had no risk of future interest rate increases? Second, why did mortgage lenders and investors not factor in rising rates when estimating the future probability of ARM delinquencies? Default is costly to the holder of a mortgage, as well as the borrower. The answer to either question could be based on fundamentals or a bubble mentality.

- *The Yield Curve:* The first question — borrower choice — may be due to borrowers taking advantage of the difference between short and long-term interest rates, called the yield curve. The greater the difference between short and long term rates, the greater the incentive for a borrower to use an ARM, which is tied to short rates, rather than a fixed rate mortgage, which is tied to long rates — especially if the borrower plans to sell or refinance the house after a short period of time. The relatively wide spread between short and long rates from 2001 to 2004 may explain the popularity of ARMs earlier in the decade, but more recently the spread between short and long rates has become small, so that the rates available on ARMs are no longer much lower than fixed rate mortgages. The continuing popularity of ARMs in light of the fall in spreads since

2005 suggests that many borrowers might have been motivated by the prospect for short-term financial gain instead.

- *The Global Savings Glut:* The second question — lenders' and investors' willingness to finance — depends in part on expectations of future interest rates. In hindsight, we know that interest rates have been trending up in global markets. At the time, however, many analysts believed that a world surplus of savings would hold down interest rates. Among the proponents of this view was the current Chairman of the Federal Reserve, Ben Bernanke [6]. Economic growth in countries with high savings rates, such as China, was forecast to add to this surplus of world savings and hold down interest rates. (Note that interest rates in Japan, for example, have been near zero for almost a decade.) Financial returns for investors in real estate and MBS looked favorable when compared to prevailing interest rates and compared to the risk in stocks following the bear market of 2000-2002. Investors increasingly turned to riskier types of MBS, and these investments performed well as long as house price appreciation held down mortgage defaults.

Securitization in the Mortgage Market

Changes in the structure of mortgage financing may have contributed to market volatility. Securitization allowed mortgage lenders to bypass traditional banks. Securitization pools mortgages or other debts and sells them to investors in the form of bonds rather than leaving loans on lenders' balance sheets. The MBS market developed in part because long-term fixed rate mortgages held in banks' portfolios place banks at significant risk if interest rates rise (in which case, the banks' interest costs could exceed their mortgage interest earnings) [7]. MBS were popular with investors and banks because it allowed both to better diversify their portfolios. But because the MBS market was growing rapidly in size and sophistication, accurate pricing of its risk was difficult and could have been distorted by the housing boom.

There are several forms of MBS. The simplest are called pass-throughs — interest and principal payments from homeowners are collected by the lender (or a service firm) and passed through to the owner of the MBS. More complex securities are created by pooling MBS as well as mortgages, and by giving investors a menu of risk and return options. A mortgage pool may be split into parts (called tranches) to allow cautious investors to purchase safer portions and aggressive investors to purchase the riskier, high-return tranches (e.g., tranches that bear initial losses). Finally, mortgage cash flows may be combined with derivative instruments that link payment levels to the performance of financial variables, such as interest rates or credit conditions. These securities — combinations of traditional bonds and derivatives — are called structured products.

The growth of securitization meant that more loans could be originated by nonbanks, [8] many of which are not subject to examination by federal bank examiners and not subject to the underwriting guidances issued by federal financial regulators. Studies of loans securitized in 2005 outside federal lending oversight suggest that the average subprime debt-to-income ratio rose to 40%, well above prudent levels in federal guidances. As the 2/28 or 3/27 loans with interest-only (I/O) periods and adjustable interest rates reset their monthly payments in 2007, many borrowers have been unable to meet their now higher monthly payment, while falling prices make it difficult to sell the house except at a loss. Forecasts of the coming resets suggest that the problem is likely to worsen in the second half of 2007 and the first half of 2008. The fall of 2008, however, is forecast to have far fewer reset problems because underwriting guidelines tightened significantly starting in August 2005.

Financial Problems for Lenders

One of the first signs that the slowdown in house price appreciation could have wider financial effects was the early stress on mortgage originators. As discussed above, securitization facilitated specialty non-bank mortgage lenders that operate outside the banking reserve system. Beginning in late 2006, some of these non-bank mortgage lenders suffered significant losses and their lines of credit began to dry up. For example, Ownit Mortgage reportedly could not cover its early payment defaults, which triggered a promise by Ownit to repurchase the nonperforming loans [9] Lenders such as Ownit depend on continuing loan sales to replenish their lines of credit and issue new mortgages. As subprime delinquency and defaults continued to rise in early 2007, the willingness of investors and securitizers to purchase mortgages from non-bank originators declined and lines of credit began to disappear. Subprime lending contracted severely and at least 90 lenders have gone out of business since the beginning of the year [10].

TURMOIL IN FINANCIAL MARKETS

A significant downturn in the housing market would be expected to cause economic distress among mortgage lenders, homeowners who expected to refinance, sellers, and related sectors such as construction. But it is not inevitable that even a severe disruption in housing should lead to a crisis in the broad financial market. In the summer of 2007, however, the global credit markets suffered a "liquidity crunch" that went well beyond the mortgage market, and the relatively small subprime segment of the market where stresses were concentrated up to then. As Federal Reserve Chairman Ben Bernanke noted, "[a]lthough this episode appears to have been triggered largely by heightened concerns about subprime mortgages, global financial losses have far exceeded even the most pessimistic projections of credit losses on those loans" [11].

In retrospect, it appears that easy credit (caused by the "saving glut") and underestimation of risk were not confined to the mortgage market. Spreads between risky corporate debt (such as junk bonds issued to finance takeovers) and safe obligations like U.S. Treasury securities were very low by historical standards — investors were willing to take risks without demanding correspondingly high interest rates in return. With both stocks and traditional fixed-income markets producing low yields after 2001, pension funds and other institutional investors were driven by their actuarial needs and competition to seek out higher-yielding investments, creating a market for hedge funds and other investment managers using exotic and complex securities and strategies. Long-term rates did not rise much even after the Federal Reserve began raising the federal funds (overnight) rate in 2004, implying that the market anticipated a plentiful supply of credit to continue into the future. This perception may have encouraged the overuse of leverage, or borrowed money, to boost returns. For example, until August, leveraged buy-outs (corporate takeovers heavily financed by debt) had soared in recent years.

A financial market adjustment need not cause widespread disruptions. Lenders could tighten their standards, debt holders could re-price their securities to reflect an updated view of risk and take the balance-sheet losses, and reckless speculators could simply go out of business, all without interrupting the mainstream of credit flows that support the global economy. But instead of such an orderly adjustment, financial markets experienced what various observers have called a rout, a panic, a crash, a bursting bubble, or a crunch. Losses have already exceeded even pessimistic expectations, as Chairman Bernanke noted, and there may be more to come. The rest of this section examines how liquidity problems spread through the financial system in August 2007.

Problems for Hedge Funds and Investment Banks

In mid-June 2007, the investment banking firm Bear Stearns announced that two of its hedge funds that invested heavily in subprime MBS were in difficulty. The securities were estimated to have lost 28% of their value since the beginning of the year. Although the funds held only about $600 million in investor capital, a negligible amount in terms of the whole U.S. mortgage market, the announcement caused alarm for several reasons.

First, the MBS held by the funds had been originally classified as very safe and low-risk by the bond rating agencies [12]. The revelation that they had lost much of their value over a very short period raised doubts about the ratings of all similar bonds, and appeared to confirm what many believed: that during the boom, many market participants had significantly underestimated the risks of lending. The announcement suggested that other holders of subprime MBS might be experiencing similar, but as yet undisclosed, losses. Thus, traders and lenders became less willing to deal with any fund or financial institution known (or suspected) to be a holder of subprime MBS. Additionally, there is a large credit derivatives market for MBS, multiplying the prospects for losses stemming from MBS volatility [13].

Second, although (as noted above) the interest rates on subprime MBS are relatively high compared to other debt securities, they do not by themselves provide the kind of returns that hedge fund investors expect. Therefore, hedge funds commonly use leverage — borrowed funds and derivative instruments — to boost returns. This means that losses in hedge funds are not only a problem for their investors — who by law must be wealthy individuals or financial institutions presumably able to bear risk and loss — but for their creditors and counterparties as well. (The Bear Stearns funds had borrowed about $6 billion from other firms, including Merrill Lynch, Goldman Sachs, Bank of America, and Deutsche Bank.) Since hedge funds are unregulated and do not disclose their sources of funds, this created uncertainty about which institutions were exposed to credit risk from hedge funds. Many derivatives markets are also largely unregulated, which means that the identities of a hedge fund's counterparties are not widely known. Thus, the Bear Stearns announcement led many to infer that other hedge funds were likely facing difficulties (which proved to be the case) and raised uncertainty about which associated brokers, lenders, and derivatives dealers might also face losses.

The Liquidity Crunch

Firms are said to be liquid when they are able to meet current obligations or short-term demand for funds. A firm is said to be solvent but illiquid when its assets exceed its liabilities but it is unable to liquidate assets rapidly enough to meet current obligations. Markets are said to be liquid when a large volume of financial securities can be traded without price distortions because there is a ready and willing supply of buyers and sellers. Liquid markets are a sign of normalcy — typically, investors can take liquidity for granted.

On August 9, 2007, liquidity abruptly dried up for many firms and securities markets. Suddenly some firms were able to borrow and investors were able to sell certain securities only at prohibitive rates and prices, if at all. The liquidity crunch was most extreme for firms and securities with links to subprime mortgages, but it also spread rapidly into seemingly unrelated areas. The apparent triggers for this liquidity crunch were losses related to U.S. housing at a French and a German bank, which followed on the Bear Stearns hedge fund announcement discussed above. Clearly, losses at two European banks alone would not be enough to cause a global liquidity crunch. Rather, news of these losses led to a sudden change in expectations among market participants that made them unwilling to lend to firms or buy securities at prevailing rates and prices. Beyond the sudden undesirability of firms and securities related to subprime mortgages, there was a general increase in risk aversion — investors suddenly required a much higher premium in order to be induced to hold risky assets — and a corresponding "flight to quality." This may be seen in the sudden plunge in the yields on 3-month Treasury bills, shown in Figure 3. Typically, three-month Treasury yields are relatively close to the federal funds rate, since overnight bank lending is also considered to have very little risk. On August 20, three-month Treasury yields were more than two percentage points below the federal funds rate.

Throughout August, there were reports of problems in other markets and financial institutions around the world, often with no apparent or previously-known connection to subprime mortgages. Although initial losses were reported in high- risk operations like hedge funds, many of the later headlines involved markets generally thought of as stable and low-risk:

- *Commercial paper*, often referred to as "corporate IOUs," is a substitute for short-term bank borrowing. Some commercial paper is backed by assets, including mortgages. The market for mortgage-backed commercial paper dried up, causing liquidity strains for issuers and various financing vehicles and conduits, some of which are owned by banks. During the flight to quality, investors became reluctant to buy any commercial paper from issuers other than the highest-rated.

- *Money market* funds are considered safe; they invest in very short- term securities. In July, there was an influx of money (over $1 trillion, by some accounts) into the funds. In August, however, several funds were revealed to be holding mortgage-backed commercial paper, and there was a surge in withdrawals, not limited to the named funds. Some funds froze redemptions rather than be forced to liquidate assets at prices they believed to be temporarily driven far below fundamental values.
- *Alt-A and jumbo mortgages* are non-conforming loans to borrowers normally considered less risky than subprime homebuyers [14]. In August, however, aversion to risk spread into these sectors of the mortgage market, as investors became less willing to purchase any MBS not issued (and guaranteed) by Fannie Mae or Freddie Mac. This caused interest rates on mortgages that those institutions could not purchase to rise, and led to calls to remove legal and regulatory limits on Fannie and Freddie's ability to buy mortgages [15]. Doubts about the solvency of mortgage lenders grew, including Countrywide Financial, the nation's largest [16].

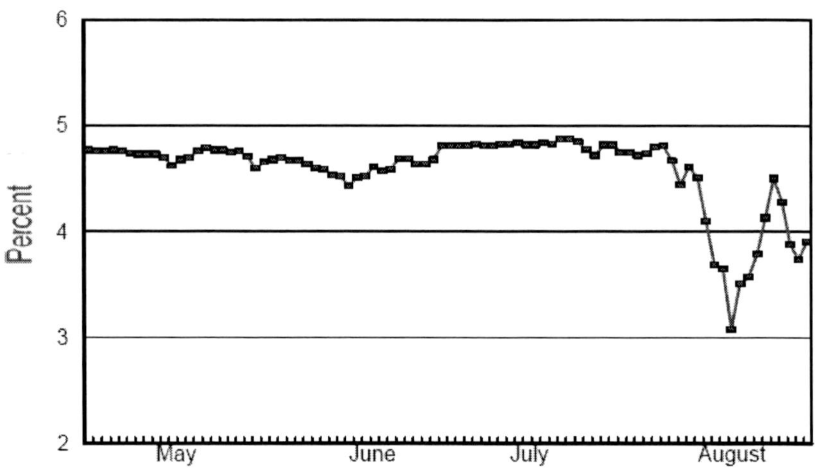

Source: Global Financial Data.

Figure 3. Yields on 3-Month Treasury Bills, May 1-August 31, 2007.

Another set of market participants subject to a sudden reevaluation were private equity firms. Over the past several years, private equity has had a strong track record of earning high profits by buying companies, restructuring their finances and operations, and reselling them to public investors. They attracted billions in capital from conservative investors like pension funds and nonprofits. Their deals depend heavily on borrowed funds, which suddenly became scarce, causing stress not only for the funds themselves, but for the institutions that had promised intermediate bridge financing for deals already in the pipeline. Private equity purchases of stock are widely believed to have been a strong factor in the recovery of the stock market since 2002; similarly, the retrenchment may have negative impact.

Turmoil in the debt markets was soon reflected in the stock market. Figure 4 shows daily highs and lows for the Dow from April 25, 2007, when the index closed above 13,000 for the first time, through the end of August. As Figure 4 illustrates, volatility increased markedly: triple-digit movements up or down in the Dow Jones Industrial Average became common, and the upward momentum seen earlier in the year, which had sent prices to record levels, was lost. Many stock markets abroad showed similar losses, although their housing markets are typically at very different cyclical positions. Price volatility produced another set of victims: hedge funds and others using computer models to trade on short-term price swings. The models could not cope with the whipsawing prices in July and August, and several "quant funds" failed.

Each of these phenomena can be plausibly explained in terms of fundamental financial conditions and factors affecting the particular markets or firms involved. What may be more important, however, is the cumulative effect they had on market psychology and, ultimately, behavior. During August, market participants did not have leisure to analyze the fundamentals behind each new headline, and the professional appraisers of risk, such as the rating agencies, appeared less trustworthy with each new revelation. Thus, to many investors and creditors, the sequence of events began to seem more and more the product an overarching panic, or contagion. Financial contagion is said to occur when financial shocks are transmitted — from firm to firm, market to market, or country to country — in a way that does not appear to be explained by fundamental supply or demand linkages.

Lawrence Summers, former Secretary of the Treasury, put it this way: "as investors rush for the exits, the focus of risk analysis shifts from fundamentals to investor behavior" [17] If investors believe that other investors are likely to sell, they have a strong incentive to sell even assets they believe are undervalued. As prices fall, collateral demands and margin calls force more selling, leading to cascading liquidations and a market crash.

A key issue for whether the liquidity crunch has lasting economic effects will depend on whether it becomes (or already has become) a credit crunch, which is defined as a situation where creditworthy borrowers are unable to borrow at all on terms that are consistent with economic fundamentals [18]. When the panic is on, the fundamentals do not matter. When asset prices fall sharply, creditors become fearful not only about the value of their collateral, but about the solvency of their borrowers. According to a Moody's economist, "a big problem is that lenders don't know which of their clients is likely to default because the system is so opaque, so they stop lending to everybody"[19]. From a policy perspective, higher risk premia may be a warranted market adjustment, but a true credit crunch could be problematic were it to emerge since it could reduce economic output.

The Response of Central Banks

Central banks across the world, including Europe, Japan, and the United States acted quickly to restore liquidity to the financial system following August 9. One sign of the liquidity crunch could be seen in the U.S. federal funds market, a private market where banks borrow and lend reserves to each other on an overnight basis. The Federal Reserve implements its policy decisions by targeting the federal funds rate; since the federal funds rate is determined by supply and demand in the federal funds market, the federal funds rate will only match the Fed's target if the Fed supplies as many or few reserves to the federal funds market as are needed (a process referred to as open market operations) [20]. To add or subtract reserves from the federal funds market, the Fed buys or sells U.S. Treasury securities.

On a normal day, the Fed might need to buy or sell a couple billion dollars of Treasury securities to keep the federal funds rate within a few one-hundredths of a percent of its target. Suddenly on August 9, the federal funds rate approached 6%, and the Fed was forced to purchase $24 billion of Treasury securities in order to add enough liquidity to bring the federal funds rate back down to its target of 5.25%. On August 10, the Fed needed to purchase an additional $38 billion to keep the rate at its target, and issued a statement that began, "The Federal Reserve is providing liquidity to facilitate the orderly functioning of financial markets." The European Central Bank provided 156 billion euros ($215 billion) of liquidity to markets on August 9 and 10. Normalcy soon returned to the federal funds market, although other parts of the financial system remained illiquid.

How should the Fed's actions of August 9 and 10 be characterized? The Fed's actions cannot be classified as a policy change since it left the federal funds target rate unchanged for over a month [21]. Nor can it be considered unusual that the Fed bought Treasury securities to keep the federal funds rate at its target — the Fed does this on a daily basis. What was unusual about the incident was the initial sharp increase in the federal funds rate above its target, and the magnitude of liquidity the Fed needed to add to bring the rate back down to its target.

On August 17, the Fed took further actions to restore calm to financial markets when it reduced the discount rate at which banks can borrow directly from the Fed from 6.25% to 5.75%. The change in the discount rate might seem unusual since the liquidity crunch does not seem to be concentrated in the sector (depository institutions) with discount window access. It is believed, however, that banks extended lines of credit and bridge financing to many of the entities suffering from the liquidity crunch, so the extent of the banking sector's exposure to the crunch is still unclear. In any case, discount window lending is dwarfed by open market operations.

On September 18, the Fed reduced the federal funds target rate by 0.5 percentage points to 4.75%, stating that the change was "intended to forestall some of the adverse effects on the broader economy that might otherwise arise from the disruptions in financial markets...." At the same time, the Fed lowered the discount rate to 5.25%.

Why Did It Happen?

There are two ways to think about the causes of financial market disorder. First, recent events can be seen as part of the standard narrative of cycles endemic to credit markets: during periods of relative stability, lenders become complacent and gradually overconfident, and the profit motive increasingly pushes aside the fear of loss. Then the credit boom comes to an end suddenly, triggered by some random event, and lenders and investors become more (and perhaps overly) cautious. Then the cycle begins again.

Financial markets had been unusually calm for a sustained period prior to August's events. The prolonged period of low and smooth interest rates was probably responsible for the notable widespread drop in risk premia, as investors may have been lulled into a false sense of confidence. History suggests that this period of placidity would inevitably end at some point. Once rates rose and became morevolatile, investors' tolerance for risk diminished. Changes in investor sentiment can be sudden and seemingly disproportionate to the proximate causes of the change. In such circumstances, investors may even take positions that are based more on their perceptions of herd behavior (e.g., selling an asset in anticipation of a panic) than underlying fundamentals. Investors may take liquidity for granted until the rare occasion when it unexpectedly disappears. When markets have been calm for a sustained period, liquidity premia tend to fall, and when it dries up, the price of less liquid assets may suddenly fall. In a liquidity crisis, firms may be forced to sell assets for less than their fundamental value to stave off insolvency.

Second, many observers attribute the current episode to additional factors that are byproducts of the ways that markets and institutions have evolved over the last few decades. Low interest rates made highly leveraged positions relatively more profitable, and highly leveraged market participants have grown quickly in size and importance. Hedge funds, the proprietary trading desks of investment and commercial banks, private equity firms, and others frequently magnify their positions through borrowing, the use of derivatives, repurchase agreements, or short sales. Highly leveraged positions will generate higher positive returns on average, but also have more potential for generating large losses. Large or unexpected losses by highly-leveraged institutions can have widespread consequences. As the President's Working Group on Financial Markets noted in its 1999 report on the Long-Term Capital Management hedge fund near-collapse,

> When leveraged investors are overwhelmed by market or liquidity shocks, the risks they have assumed will be discharged back into the market. Thus, highly leveraged investors have the potential to exacerbate instability in the market as a whole. The outcome may be direct losses inflicted on creditors and trading counterparties, as well as an indirect impact on other market participants through price changes resulting from the disappearance of investors willing to bear higher risks. The indirect impact is potentially the more serious effect. Volatility and sharp declines in asset prices can heighten uncertainty about credit risk and disrupt the intermediation of credit. These secondary effects, if not contained, could cause a contraction of credit and liquidity, and ultimately, heighten the risk of a contraction in real economic activity [22].

Much financial intermediation has migrated from the banks — which are closely supervised and insured by federal regulators — to lightly or unregulated non-banks, and as a result the financial system has become more opaque. Similarly, the use of ever more complex financial instruments — derivatives, CDOs, structured products, etc. — both permits risks to be transferred quickly from one market or institution to another and makes it difficult to discern where the ultimate risk exposure lies. For example, MBS investors have had difficulty telling whether the mortgages underlying their securities are at risk. This opacity is not a problem when markets are functioning smoothly, and indeed the consensus view is that the ability to unbundle and transfer risk has made the financial system more robust and efficient. But the downside is that when losses do occur there is greater uncertainty about who might be affected and the extent of the damage, potentially leading to greater panic.

Some economists have speculated that the growing complexity of and turnover in financial markets can exacerbate rare periods of extreme volatility. For example, when highly leveraged positions go sour, the process of unwinding those positions can drive asset prices even further down. Highly sophisticated hedges based on assets that are normally uncorrelated may suddenly become correlated during episodes of instability. For example, a hedge based on the assumption that two asset prices will not fall simultaneously could become costly to unwind if all prices are falling. Liquidity is crucial for many of these transactions to work — when it disappears, they fall apart. Relatively new classes of securities may have too short a history for a comprehensive knowledge of their risk profile, so that unexpected events lead to a sudden and dramatic repricing of the securities.

As discussed above, the downturn in the housing market has been unfolding for some time, and it was always likely that it would result in financial market adjustment for securities related to the housing market. Perhaps what was surprising was how sudden and extreme that adjustment turned out to be, although asset bubbles have often burst suddenly. At this point, the adjustment seems to be based more on anticipation of a future (rather than actual) rise in mortgage delinquencies, and so actual delinquencies could turn out to be higher or lower than current financial markets reflect. (The recent increase in subprime delinquencies remains a small portion of the total mortgage market.) If so, there will be further financial market adjustment, for better or worse.

What is not yet clear is whether recent events (which were much more broadly based than just the mortgage market) will lead to permanent changes in asset pricing due to a change in underlying fundamentals, or whether recent financial losses are mostly the result of panic and will eventually be reversed as calm is restored. To a large extent, this question revolves around whether permanent financial adjustment is limited to the mortgage market or whether the mortgage market represents the proverbial "tip of the iceberg."

It could prove to be the latter if the period of a "global liquidity glut" and low risk premia was an aberration that has come to a close. Data suggest that low global interest rates were always being driven more by low investment demand than high saving [23]. If so, it was always likely that investment demand would eventually recover, and, when it did, interest rates would be driven up.

POLICY ISSUES

The liquidity crunch of August 2007 raises a number of policy issues. The fundamental question underlying them is whether the crunch and the current policy approach to its resolution has exposed the economy to an acceptable level of risk. If the liquidity crunch leaves no lasting harm, and the policy response (mainly, the Fed's attempt to replenish the financial system's lost liquidity) is effective and has no negative side effects, then some would argue that the natural ups and downs of financial markets are a useful and necessary way to ensure that capital is allocated efficiently. In the famous words of Joseph Schumpeter, the credit crunch may represent capitalism's "creative destruction." But the 2007 credit crunch has raised issues in a number of policy areas where economists have questioned whether policy changes could have averted the crunch, or at least tempered its more destructive side effects, without undermining market efficiency.

The first part of this section evaluates the macroeconomic response, namely the efficacy of the Fed's current approach to provide liquidity to financial markets when it dries up. The rest of the section focuses on regulatory issues that have been raised by August's events — the fear of financial contagion, finding the proper degree of regulation for modern financial markets, and potential shortcomings with rating agencies and the regulation of mortgage markets — with an eye on preventing their reoccurrence. Finally, to understand why a liquidity crunch merits policymakers' attention, the chapter links financial unrest to its ultimate effect on the real economy.

Monetary Policy in a Liquidity Crunch

With the potential to flood the market with virtually unlimited amounts of money, the Fed can in effect offset any loss in overall liquidity in financial markets [24]. But adding too much liquidity would undermine the Fed's long-term goals of maintaining low inflation and stable economic growth. So when faced with financial unrest, the Fed's options for restoring calm in the short-term are constrained by its unwillingness to undermine its long-term goals. Since monetary changes feed through to inflation only gradually, the faster excess liquidity is withdrawn after calm is restored to financial markets, the less of a threat it poses to low inflation.

If a liquidity crunch is the market outcome resulting from the decisions of private investors, why should the Fed intervene? Some have argued that when the

Fed does restore liquidity, it increases moral hazard, the economic term for the idea that people take greater risks when they are insured against adverse outcomes. In this case, in the words of the head of Britain's central bank, "The (recent) provision of such liquidity support undermines the efficient pricing of risk by providing ex-post insurance for risky behavior. That encourages excessive risk-taking and sows the seeds of a future crisis" [25]. These critics argue that more efficient investment decisions would be made in the long run if the Fed allowed liquidity crunches to run their course and imprudent investors took losses [26].

The effectiveness of the Fed's efforts to restore liquidity is limited by the fact that the Fed's actions only affect market liquidity at the broadest level. As long as investors shun classes of borrowers or assets, those markets will remain illiquid and out of line with underlying fundamentals. As a result, monetary policy cannot make all markets function smoothly all the time. This reduces moral hazard, however, since it means that the Fed's actions do not interfere with market rewards and punishments for specific risk-taking behavior.

The drawback to the moral hazard critique is that allowing a liquidity crunch to run its course could run counter to the Fed's long-run goal of maintaining economic stability. If the liquidity crunch were to lead to recession, not only would overly risky investors take losses, but so would efficient firms that saw demand for their products drop solely because of the cyclical downturn. Some would argue that liquidity has characteristics of a positive externality, whose benefits to society exceed the benefits to private firms who provide it. If so, enough liquidity can be provided only through government intervention, in this case by the Fed.

Although the positive externality argument is generally consistent with mainstream economic thought, it and the moral hazard critique are not mutually exclusive. Traditionally, government programs that create moral hazard are complemented by government regulations to reduce risky behavior. For example, deposit insurance creates the incentive for banks to take on excessive risk, so bank regulations restrict the amount of risk that banks are allowed to take. As will be discussed below, if moral hazard really is being created by the Fed, there may not currently be corresponding regulations to offset the extra risk it generates.

The decision to lower rates is similar to the 1998 experience. Similar to today, the U.S. economy had been experiencing a sustained expansion when financial turmoil suddenly erupted in September 1998 in response to the Russian debt default, the second round of Asian crises, and financial difficulties at a hedge fund called Long-Term Capital Management [27]. In response, the Fed cut interest rates by 0.25 percentage points on three separate occasions over the next two months, then held rates constant until June 1999. Following these actions, calm was restored and the economic expansion and bull market continued for another two years. In hindsight, some economists have argued that cutting interest rates in 1998 was the wrong decision, because it caused the economy to overheat, inflation to rise, and a stock market bubble to grow. They argue that the economic downturn and stock market decline that began in 2001 could have been mitigated had the Fed not acted in 1998 [28].

Systemic Risk and Contagion

The events of August are an example of financial contagion, which occurs when financial shocks are not confined to the markets where they originate, but are transmitted to other firms, markets, or countries with no fundamental link to the original problem. Trouble in the U.S. subprime mortgage market has triggered systemic risk, or repercussions throughout the global financial system. Is systemic risk too high in today's financial system? If so, what options do policy makers have to reduce the incidence of contagion, or systemic risk?

In general, markets are self-correcting and self-stabilizing. The price mechanism ensures that when asset prices fall far enough, new buyers will be found and a new equilibrium established. In the United States, some of the largest financial markets — trading in foreign exchange and U.S. Treasury securities, for example — have functioned very well with virtually no government regulation.

True systemic risk episodes are rare events, and when they do occur, there may not be significant damage to the real economy. It is impossible to know whether instances where the Fed has successfully stepped in to quell financial turmoil, such as October 1998 and August 2007, were narrowly averted "near misses" or whether calm would have been restored anyway without government intervention. Nevertheless, financial regulators spend considerable time thinking about worst-case scenarios, because of the possible severity of the macroeconomic consequences. In the United States, modern banking and securities regulation both have their roots in and derive their basic principles from the lessons of the Great Depression, when the stock market crash of 1929 and a banking panic accompanied a decade of economic contraction and stagnation.

In economic terms, systemic risk is an externality to individual market participants. All firms have an incentive to limit their own risk taking to avoid a loss of their capital, but none has an adequate incentive to limit risk taking to reduce instability in the system at large. In the recent housing boom, decisions made by individual borrowers and lenders may have been entirely reasonable given the information available at the time, but, at the systemic level, those choices produced an unstable situation.

Should financial regulators try to reduce systemic risk by setting limits on private risk taking? There are difficulties in this approach. First, if regulators want to mandate that market participants hold more capital as a cushion to enable them to better withstand financial shocks, no one knows how much additional stability any given capital increase will yield. The problem is analogous to writing earthquake insurance policies: with a low-frequency, high-severity event, there is not enough historical data to support a robust model of the likely cost of the next unlikely occurrence. Prudential regulation imposes costs, but the systemic benefits are uncertain.

Second, financial markets are extremely dynamic, creating a moving target for regulatory attempts to reduce systemic risk. In recent years, there has been a massive movement of capital out of regulated entities like mutual funds and banks, into unregulated hedge funds and private equity. The spread of new instruments to manage, unbundle, and redistribute risk has been noted above. Furthermore, in modern financial markets, assets may be held for very brief periods of time, making regulation technically difficult. Where innovation is rapid, risk models can quickly become outdated is to rely on the Federal Reserve to step in after the fact, to provide liquidity, and, if need be, to act as lender of last resort to bail out institutions whose failure would have unacceptable systemic consequences. As discussed in the previous section, the main drawback of this approach is the potential for moral hazard to increase.

Could Problems in the Mortgage Market Have Been Averted?

Several factors contributed to the housing boom and bust, and only time will tell which factors played the largest role. In hindsight, many borrowers took on loans that were unsustainable, especially loans with introductory rates and interest-only periods, whose use peaked in 2005. Evidence shows that loans originated by banks subject to federal safety and soundness regulators were more likely to maintain prudent underwriting [29]. The non-bank lenders, in contrast, appear to have been more likely to extend imprudent loans. Potential reasons on both the borrowing and lending side could include

- relative lack of financial sophistication by borrowers in the subprime market, which is disproportionately conducted by non-banks;

- deceptive or misleading loan marketing techniques by mortgage brokers and lenders with little long-term financial interests in loan performance;
- inflated appraisals during high refinance periods by appraisers seeking repeat business;
- weak underwriting criteria of lenders speculating on continued house price appreciation to hold down defaults;
- insufficient data and weak default models used by ratings agencies to estimate financial risks; and
- lack of due diligence by overconfident investors in mortgage backed securities.

Each factor suggests a different, but not mutually exclusive, response. Better financial education and improved disclosure laws, which would apply to both bank and non-bank lenders, might have improved the judgment of borrowers who took out unsustainable loans. Improved supervision of mortgage brokers and lenders could have resulted in tighter lending standards. More accurate and objective estimations by parties paid for their opinion, such as appraisers and ratings agencies, could have led to a more accurate pricing of value and risk, which would minimize the current need for a correction. More prudent underwriting standards among non-banks, either through better due diligence by securities investors or regulation by federal bank examiners, could have reduced the volume of unsustainable loans. The latter option would mark a break from current policy.

Although federal disclosure laws apply to all mortgages, not all lenders are subject to federal scrutiny for safety and soundness. Federal financial regulators concerned for the safety and soundness of the banking system issue guidances that encourage prudent lending. These guidances do not apply to many subprime and jumbo loan lenders that choose to securitize their loans. The underwriting standards of these lenders depend on the willingness of investors in MBS to purchase the loans. While house price appreciation was holding down defaults, MBS securities performed well, investment demand for them was strong, and underwriting standards loosened. Average debt-to-income ratio for subprime loans, for example, rose from 36% in 1998 to 40% in 2005. It appears at this time that problem loans originated disproportionately in the unregulated channel.

When considering whether non-bank mortgage lenders should face the same regulatory scrutiny as banks, it is useful to recall the purpose of bank regulation. Because of deposit insurance, banks face little scrutiny from depositors regarding the riskiness of their lending. "Safety and soundness" bank regulation reduces risk, and thereby the costs of deposit insurance, in the face of moral hazard. It was not meant to protect borrowers. The traditional rationale for why other financial institutions face less regulation than banks is because they face nothing analogous to the moral hazard created by deposit insurance.

Financial Market Regulation

According to Axel Weber, president of the German central bank, "the current turmoil ... has all the characteristics of a classic banking crisis, but one that is taking place outside the traditional banking sector" [30] In pre-deposit insurance days, if one bank got in trouble, depositors at the bank across the street would line up to withdraw their money, not because they had new information about the condition of their own bank, but simply as a precautionary measure: the cost of withdrawing funds was minimal; the cost of waiting too long might be high. What is happening now, in Weber' s analysis, is comparable, except that instead of banks, the affected institutions are mainly conduits and investment vehicles raising funds in the corporate bond market. These institutions have borrowed short-term (e.g., using commercial paper) to finance long-term investments (MBS), and they are as vulnerable to runs as a bank (in the absence of deposit insurance) with illiquid assets (loans) financed by short-term borrowing (deposits). Most notably in the case of subprime MBS, some of the assets are now at higher risk of default, but investors are having difficulty telling which ones, so they are avoiding the entire asset class. One of the original rationales for banking regulation was to reduce the cyclicality of the credit markets, and other parts of the financial sector have shown themselves to be no less prone to cyclicality.

Hedge funds, non-bank mortgage lenders, private equity firms, issuers of commercial paper, and their ancillary credit suppliers have also faced liquidity problems as investors have sought to move into safer, more liquid assets. A policy question is whether certain non-bank financial institutions ought to be brought under the federal safety net, in exchange for accepting some form of prudential regulation. A problem with the current approach is that the Federal Reserve can only inject liquidity into the financial system through the banking sector. If banks are under stress — one estimate is that they have had to take $1.3 trillion in risky assets back onto their balance sheets in recent months [31] — they may not be in a position to pass liquidity to the non-bank sectors that most need it. According to one commentator, the Federal Reserve could in that situation find itself "pushing on a string" [32]. The objections to widening the safety net, based on the concept of moral hazard, are discussed above. But even if the federal safety net were not extended, an argument for extending regulation could be made based on the moral hazard created by the Federal Reserve's actions to maintain liquidity.

Large hedge funds. The word "opaque" appears often in writing about the current liquidity crunch, including this chapter: perhaps more disclosure by currently unregulated financial institutions would reduce uncertainty. As noted above, a key motivation for the recent "flight to quality" appears to be that investors are unable to tell whether the assets they are holding are in danger. Investors might be expected to demand greater disclosure in return for the use of their funds, but at least until August, investment was migrating to sectors with the least disclosure. The limitation to increasing disclosure is that it is most useful when financial positions are relatively simple and stable: when they are dynamic and complex, disclosed information becomes rapidly outdated.

Rating Agencies

Bond rating agencies, of which Moody's and Standard and Poor's are the best-known, are private firms that assign grades to debt securities, indicative of the raters' estimates of the probability that interest and principal will be paid on schedule. The rating agencies have been of interest to Congress since the Enron collapse, when bonds of many companies were not downgraded until long after their management and accounting problems had become public knowledge. Congress passed the Credit Rating Agency Reform Act of 2006 (P.L. 109-291) to address the perceived problems created by the absence of statutory regulation of credit rating agencies [33]. The act attempts to increase competition in the rating industry, by making it easier for an agency to obtain Securities and Exchange Commission (SEC) certification. The SEC, however, does not exercise any direct regulatory supervision over the rating agencies.

In 2007, the rating agencies have been widely blamed for missing looming problems in subprime MBS, causing first a false sense of security among investors, and then widespread insecurity as investors lost faith in rating designations.34 What are the options for additional reforms?

One approach would be new legislation to bring the rating agencies under some form of SEC regulation. The SEC could be authorized to examine (or require disclosure of) rating methodologies, and perhaps prescribe standards for revising ratings in response to new information or changes in market conditions. The SEC could also monitor possible conflicts of interest; critics have charged that the rating agencies may sometimes adjust their ratings for competitive purposes (that is, to win business from a rival by offering a more favorable rating since issuers pay for ratings), and that issuers seeking ratings may be pressured to purchase various consulting services offered by rating agency affiliates. (There have been no public allegations that such practices underlie the problems with subprime MBS ratings)

An opposing view is that efforts to improve the quality of the ratings are likely to produce only limited results. Markets react to new information quickly and continuously: is it realistic to think that rating agencies can have superior information about each of the thousands of rated debt securities? The rating agencies employ highly skilled analysts, but basic financial theory holds that no single individual or firm — or the SEC, for that matter — can do a better job of valuation than the market as a whole.

If rating agencies' decisions sole purpose was to guide private investment decisions, one could argue that questions concerning the quality of ratings were of no concern to public policy. The rating agencies are a concern, however, because many regulations hinge on an asset's rating. Among the legal consequences of a rating change may be higher capital requirements (for banks or securities broker/dealers) or forced divestment of certain assets (for example, by federally-insured thrifts that are forbidden to hold below investment grade (or "junk") debt). An alternate approach, then, would be for Congress to reconsider the numerous provisions in regulation and statute that refer to private rating decisions. Those doubting the usefulness of rating agencies might argue that the role of ratings in public policy should be diminished.

Financial Markets and the Real Economy

The overarching goals of the government's macroeconomic policies are not to prevent financial losses but to maintain low inflation and stable economic growth. As long as the financial system as a whole remains stable, losses for some investors are needed for capital to be allocated most efficiently and the economy to prosper. Maintaining some degree of financial stability is a policy goal not in and of itself, but because it is required for economic stability.

Although financial "paper losses" have no direct effect on economic output or employment, there are channels through which changes in financial conditions are transmitted to the real economy. Most importantly, physical capital investment is a key component of gross domestic product (GDP), and a firm's decision to invest in physical capital (plant or equipment) is influenced by borrowing costs, access to capital markets, and its stock price. If these three determinants deteriorate, then firms are likely to reduce their physical investment, and GDP growth would eventually fall, all else equal. Given that mortgage-related asset prices have fallen most significantly in the recent episode, any decline in physical investment may turn out to be concentrated in residential investment (house building). Even if firms and individuals would still like to borrow after a financial downturn, financial firms that have suffered losses may curb their lending to improve their balance sheets.

Another channel from which financial losses can lead to lower GDP growth is through household consumption. If household wealth declines, households may eventually increase their saving — equivalently, reduce their consumption — in order to replenish it. Consumption remained relatively strong, however, during the stock market decline from 2001 to 2003, which was much larger than recent losses to date. Households with mortgage difficulties — a small fraction of the total — may be forced to reduce consumption as a result of lost access to credit. Households may also reduce their consumption as a result of declining confidence, and financial turmoil may cause confidence to decline.

If investment or consumption were to decline, it may be partly offset by an improvement in the trade deficit. Foreign capital inflows have played an important role in financing U.S. investment spending in the past few years, and if investment spending were to fall, foreign capital inflows might also fall. By accounting identity, net foreign capital inflows are equal to the current account deficit, of which the trade deficit is the largest part. Lower net capital inflows would reduce the value of the dollar, which would make exports and import-competing goods relatively less expensive. While the trade deficit would improve, foreign capital outflows could prevent interest rates from falling, however.

As the examples of the stock market decline on October 19, 1987 — the largest single day percentage decline in history — and the financial turmoil in 1998 demonstrate, financial losses need not lead to economic recessions. Nor is the direction of causation obvious in cases where stock market declines and recessions have coincided. For example, while the stock market decline preceded the 2001 recession, it might have been caused by investors' recognition that the economy was weakening, as opposed to causing the recession itself. In general, historical experience suggests that prolonged bear markets, not transient financial unrest, are associated with recessions

References

[1] A "2/28" is an adjustable-rate mortgage where the rate is fixed for the first two years, then adjusts for each of the next 28 years. "Interest only" ARMs

have an introductory period where no principal is paid off. "Teaser rates" refer to ARMs with an introductory interest rate that is below market rates. "Option ARMs (adjustable rate mortgages)" offer homebuyers several payment options each month: interest, principal, both, or part of either.

[2] "Alt-A" most often refers to buyers who do not provide full documentation of income from traditional employment, but who would otherwise be considered prime borrowers.

[3] Inside Mortgage Finance, *2007 Mortgage Market Statistical Annual*, vol. 1, p. 3.

[4] Mark Gilbert, "Unsafe at Any Rating," *Bloomberg. Com*, August 30, 2007.

[5] Just as liquidity plays a crucial role in securities markets, liquidity is important when housing is bought for investment purposes. Investors whose financial plans are based on being able to sell a house promptly may run into difficulties when sales slow.

[6] See Ben Bernanke, "The Global Saving Glut and the U.S. Current Account Deficit," the Sandridge Lecture, Virginia Association of Economics, March 10, 2005, available on the Federal Reserve Board of Governors website. For a discussion, see CRS Report RL33 140, *Is the Trade Deficit Caused by a Global Saving Glut?*, by Marc Labonte.

[7] This was the problem behind the savings and loan crisis in the 1980s: inflation and rising interest rates required lenders to pay their depositors more than they were earning on their fixed-rate mortgage assets.

[8] For example, securitization meant that non-banks needed to obtain financing only until a mortgage was sold on the secondary market, so deposits were not needed to finance mortgages.

[9] Julie Creswell and Vikas Bajaj, "*A Mortgage Crisis Begins to Spiral and Casualties Mount,*" New York Times, March 5, 2007, p. C1.

[10] Economist Intelligence Unit, "Heading for the Rocks," August 2007, p. 13.

[11] "Housing, Housing Finance, and Monetary Policy ," Remarks by Chairman Ben S. Bernanke at the Federal Reserve Bank of Kansas City's Economic Symposium, Jackson Hole, Wyoming, August 31, 2007.

[12] Bond rating agencies, of which Moody's and Standard and Poor's are the best-known, are private firms that assign grades to debt securities, indicative of the raters' estimates of the probability that interest and principal will be paid on schedule. The ratings are important not only to investors trying to select a portfolio that matches their risk preferences, but they are also written into many federal laws and regulations. For example, the amount of regulatory capital banks are required to hold to cover the risk of loss to their bond holdings is determined by the rating assigned by the agencies, and

thrift institutions are not allowed to own bonds rated below investment grade. In 2007, many blame the rating agencies for failing to downgrade subprime MBS in a timely way in response to negative information about rising defaults and imminent resets that became available early in the year.

[13] Credit derivatives are essentially bets that a debt security or firm will default, be downgraded by a rating agency, or experience another "credit event." They provide insurance for bondholders, and speculative opportunities for those who believe that the bonds' credit quality are deteriorating.

[14] Jumbo loans are non-conforming because they are larger than Fannie Mae and Freddie Mac are allowed to purchase.

[15] See. e.g., Lawrence Summers, "This Is Where Fannie and Freddie Step In," *Financial Times*, August 27, 2007, p. 11. (Fannie and Freddie cannot buy mortgages of over $417,000, and their underwriting standards limit their purchases of Alt-A and subprime loans.)

[16] In an effort to reassure the market, Countrywide obtained a large cash infusion from Bank of America. See "Countrywide Receives $2 Billion Strategic Equity Investment From Bank Of America," Countrywide Financial Corporation Press Release, August 22, 2007.

[17] "This Is Where Fannie and Freddie Step In," *Financial Times*, August 27, 2007, p. 11.

[18] Since economic fundamentals can be difficult to accurately measure, it is harder to identify a credit crunch with confidence than a liquidity crunch.

[19] Shawn Tully, "Risk Returns With a Vengeance," *Fortune,* vol. 156, September 3, 2007: p. 50.

[20] For a primer, see CRS Report RL30354, *Monetary Policy and the Federal Reserve: Current Policy and Conditions,* by Marc Labonte and Gail Makinen

[21] Although no change in the targeted rate was announced, the Fed allowed the actual federal funds rate to fall below 5% on most days over the next month.

[22] "Hedge Funds, Leverage, and the Lessons of Long-Term Capital Management," Report of The President's Working Group on Financial Markets, April 1999, p. 23.

[23] See CRS Report RL33 140, *Is the U.S. Trade Deficit Caused by a Global Saving Glut?*, by Marc Labonte.

[24] While the Fed can increase the availability of credit, there is always the rare possibility that lenders will not use it, in which case the Fed's efforts to restore liquidity could be stymied. This scenario is referred to as a "liquidity trap."

[25] Carter Dougherty, "British Central Bank Critical of Cash Infusions," New York Times, September 13, 2007. Soon after, the British central bank appeared to reverse its stance by providing financial markets with significant liquidity.

[26] This argument should not be overstated. Investors will only be "bailed out" in instances when their losses correspond with steps by the Fed to restore liquidity, and plenty of investors still experienced losses during recent events despite the Fed's actions.

[27] See CRS Report RL30232, *Systemic Risk and the Long-Term Capital Management Rescue,* by Mark Jickling.

[28] See CRS Report RL33666, *Asset Bubbles: Policy Options for the Federal Reserve*, by Marc Labonte.

[29] Thus, there is no easy option for regulators to use to reduce the frequency of systemic crises in advance. The best available policy may be the current one, which 29 Some critics have argued that banks would have made more prudent loans if they did not Krishna Guha, "Credit Turmoil 'Has Hallmarks of Bank Run' ," *FT. Com*, September 2, 2007.

[30] Krishna Guha, "Credit Turmoil 'Has Hallmarks of Bank Run' ," *FT. Com,* September 2, 2007.

[31] Comments of Paul McCulley, managing director of Pimco, ibid. When the market for securitization dried up, banks were forced to hold loans and other debt assets that they had expected to sell. Banks also provide bridge financing for a variety of transactions, including private equity deals: when those deals are not completed, loans intended to be short-term may become long-term.

[32] Lawrence Summers, "This Is Where Fannie and Freddie Step In," *Financial Times,* August 27, 2007, p. 11.

[33] For a summary of this legislation, see CRS Report RS225 19, *Credit Rating Agency Reform Act of 2006,* by Michael V. Seitzinger.

In: Financial Crisis in America ISBN 978-1-60692-191-3
Editor: Raymond T. Ovanhouser, pp. 77-96 © 2009 Nova Science Publishers, Inc.

Chapter 3

AVERTING FINANCIAL CRISIS*

Mark Jickling

ABSTRACT

There is no precise definition of "financial crisis," but a common view is that disruptions in financial markets rise to the level of a crisis when the flow of credit to households and businesses is constrained and the real economy of goods and services is adversely affected. Since mid-2007, central bankers — including the Federal Reserve — have labored to keep the downturn in U.S. subprime housing from developing into such a crisis.

While subprime problems were widely anticipated, the subsequent spread of turmoil into many seemingly unrelated parts of the global financial system was not. Many losses occurring in diverse firms and markets — often quite severe — have features in common: the use of complex, hard-to-value financial instruments; large speculative positions underwritten by borrowed funds, or leverage; and the use of off-the-books entities to remove risky trading activities from the balance sheets of major financial institutions.

It is not yet clear whether financial market problems will significantly slow the economy: many believe that the current episode is simply the downside of a normal credit cycle, that is, a natural corrective to several years of unusually easy credit conditions. On the other hand, some analysts identify market dynamics that may amplify the effects of financial shocks and have the potential to generate self-reinforcing, downward financial and economic spirals. The Federal Reserve has used its traditional tools to avert such an outcome: it has lowered short-term interest rates dramatically and

* Excerpted from CRS Report RL34412 date march 21, 2008.

injected billions of dollars into the banking system to support market liquidity and keep credit flowing. In addition, the Fed has expanded its sphere by making funds available to securities firms, which it does not regulate, and has provided funding to underwrite the rescue-through-acquisition of Bear Stearns, a leading investment bank. The duration of the current instability is in marked contrast to financial shocks of recent decades — stock market crashes, bond market disruptions, the 9/11 attacks — when the central bank was able to contain market problems quickly with little or no interruption of U.S. economic growth.

Depending on how soon normal market conditions are restored, and at what cost, policy makers may consider whether regulators have access to adequate information about market conditions, and whether currently unregulated market participants should be subjected to disclosure and reporting requirements. In addition, the social costs of failed financial speculation may be judged great enough to warrant new restrictions designed to lower the incidence of losses that have system-wide impacts or to put the markets and the economy in a better position to weather such shocks.

This chapter supplements CRS Report RL34 182, Financial Crisis? The Liquidity Crunch of August 2007, by Darryl Getter et al., which describes in greater detail the channels through which subprime problems cascaded through the financial system. This chapter focuses on the efforts of regulators to reduce stress to the markets.

INTRODUCTION

In mid-2007, mounting losses in subprime mortgage markets triggered disturbances throughout the international financial system. The scale of the turmoil has been surprising, given the small size of the U.S. subprime market in relation to global financial markets. Not only is subprime a comparatively small market, its problems were known well in advance: when the rapid rise in housing prices stopped in 2006, it was inevitable that many subprime borrowers would have difficulty making payments, particularly those whose adjustable mortgage rates were scheduled to reset in 2007 and 2008. A Swiss bank CEO has called subprime loan losses "probably the longest anticipated crisis we have ever seen"[1].

Nevertheless, a wide range of financial institutions have been affected adversely, many of which had no direct exposure to the subprime mortgage market. Almost weekly since July 2007, the financial press has highlighted a new trouble spot, such as hedge funds, small European banks, issuers of commercial paper, conduits for securitization of loans, credit swaps, jumbo mortgages, money market funds, consumer lenders, bond insurers, state and local government investment funds, and so on. The links between many of these markets and subprime mortgages are tenuous, but they are widely viewed as symptoms of a common underlying problem.

The stock market has certainly perceived systemic weakness across financial sectors. As Figure 1 below indicates, share prices for large banks, small banks, and investment banks have all significantly underperformed the market as a whole, as represented by the Standard & Poor's 500 index. Between July 2007 and March 2008, shares in those companies lost about a third of their value.

Financial market conditions have not stabilized, despite the efforts of regulators. The ultimate fear of the Federal Reserve is that the flow of credit to sound business and consumer borrowers will be disrupted, causing spending and investment to contract sharply throughout the economy. To date, there has been "tightness" in certain lending markets, but credit remains generally available. This chapter focuses on the tools that regulators — primarily but not exclusively the Federal Reserve — have employed or devised to avert a full-blown financial crisis that would be expected to worsen macroeconomic conditions.

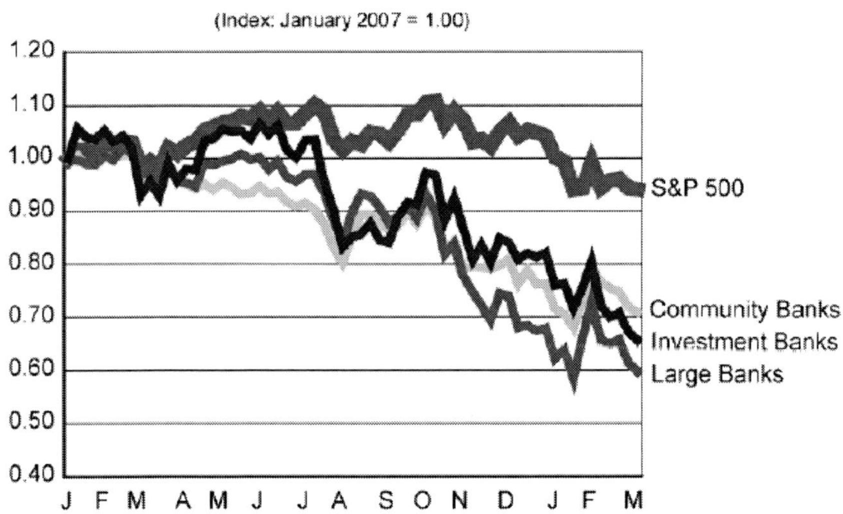

Source: Global Financial Data.

Figure 1. Commercial and Investment Bank Stock Indexes, January 2007- March 2008.

The Underlying Financial Problems

CRS Report RL34182, *Financial Crisis? The Liquidity Crunch of August 2007,* by Darryl Getter et al., describes the channels through which distress in subprime mortgages spread through the broader financial system. The subprime crisis triggered a ressessment of financial risk that encompassed other markets, including leveraged loans, [2] takeover financing, credit derivatives and commercial paper. There was — and still remains — great uncertainty regarding the true value of certain financial instruments, especially those with complex structures or for which active trading markets do not exist.

In the changed atmosphere, many market participants became reluctant to extend credit, either because they could not judge the prospective borrower's financial condition with any confidence, or because they were unsure what the assets in their own capital base would bring, should they be forced to liquidate them to cope with unexpected losses. This reluctance translated into what the Federal Reserve calls tightness, primarily in the interbank lending market, but also in certain consumer and business credit markets.

One way to describe the root problem is to call it valuation risk — the information or transparency that facilitates the smooth flow of credit was suddenly lacking. That valuation problems should have so marked an effect is a result of several long-term trends in financial markets:

- the use of complex financial instruments, whose value is often linked by complex formulae to the value of other instruments or financial variables, and for which no active trading markets exist;
- the practice of moving risky financial speculation off the books, into nominally independent accounting entities, so that the results do not appear in the financial accounts of the parent financial institution; and
- the growing use of leverage, or borrowed funds, which permits institutions to take larger market positions with a given capital base, increasing potential profits (but also losses).

One example that embodies all three trends is the Structured Investment Vehicle, or SIV, an entity created by banks to enable speculation on the relationship between short- and long-term interest rates.

SIVs

In mid-2007, commercial banks operated several dozen SIVs, with total assets of between $350 billion and $400 billion. Figure 2 illustrates the basic cash flows. The SIV bought long-term debt assets, often mortgage-backed bonds, from which it received interest income. Purchase of these assets was financed by issuing short-term debt, usually commercial paper [3]. The SIV' s net revenue was determined by the difference, or spread, between these two cash flows; the operation was profitable so long as the payouts from the assets exceeded interest payments to the commercial paper holders.

The profits were distributed in two ways: first as fees for services to the sponsoring institution, and second, as dividends or interest to holders of subordinated debt and equity, who were the nominal owners of the SIV. (Accounting rules require outside ownership for the SIV to be carried off the books of the sponsoring bank. In general, however, the bank was responsible for investment decisions and provided all brokerage, trade processing, and other services.)

According to one estimate, 72% of the equity in mortgage conduits, of which SIVs are a subset, was held by hedge funds [4]. Hedge funds are typically highly leveraged, which suggests that much of the equity capital in SIVs was borrowed, perhaps from the sponsoring banks themselves.

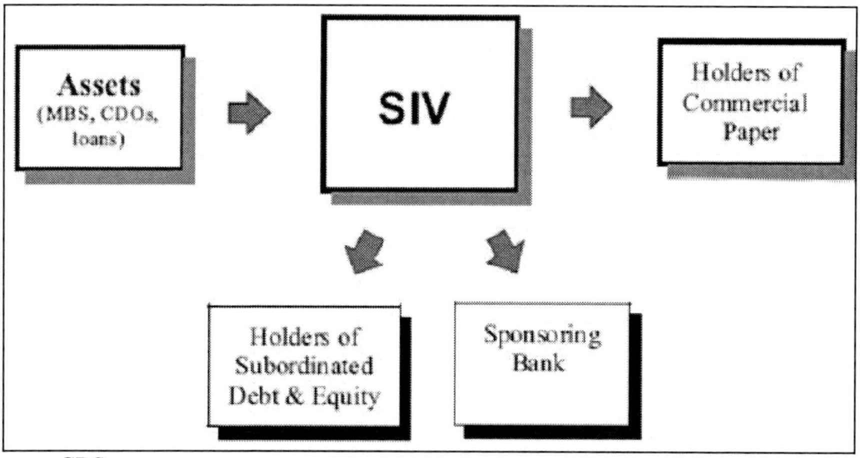

Source: CRS.

Figure 2. Structured Investment Vehicle Cash Flows.

Many of the assets held by SIVs were mortgage-related, but rarely were they actual loans. Rather, they were securities backed by pools of loans, in which the interest and principal payments of homeowners are passed through to the holders of the bonds. Financial engineers also bundled mortgage-backed bonds into pools of securities called collateralized debt obligations (CDOs), and sold claims against them. CDOs were carved into various classes with different risk characteristics and yields. The portions of the pool that proved most difficult to sell might be pooled again, carved up, and resold — in a so-called CDO squared.

Despite their complexity, such securities were often able to obtain AAA ratings, despite the fact that they were offering interest rates significantly higher than AAA corporate bonds. CDOs found a ready market in institutional investors seeking higher yields than traditional debt instruments offered in the early 2000s, and they were incorporated into aggressive speculative strategies such as SIVs.

As subprime defaults climbed to historically unprecedented levels in 2007, the value of mortgage-backed instruments became hard to determine, since it depended crucially on uncertain projections of future loan performance. CDOs were particularly affected, since by the time loans had been pooled and resold two or three times, it was difficult for investors to ascertain exactly what they owned.

SIVs found that they were no longer able to sell the commercial paper that supported their assets. Sponsoring banks were required to extend credit to the SIVs (and in many cases were compelled to do so, having granted contingent lines of credit in order to secure high ratings for their SIVs' commercial paper) or to take the assets onto their own balance sheets, exacerbating their own financial difficulties. Major banks did not allow SIVs to fail because of the reputational damage that would follow, but the associated losses were considerable.

SIVs are only one part of the story of liquidity problems in 2007 and 2008, but they are instructive because they include three features that contributed disturbance elsewhere. First, they involved the use of innovative securities, which were hard to value in the best of circumstances and which had little history to indicate how they might behave in a severe market downturn. Second, risks were underestimated: theSIVs were a form of highly-leveraged speculation, which was dependent on the assumption that the markets would always supply liquidity. Finally, they were off balance sheet entities: few in the markets (or perhaps in the regulatory agencies) had an accurate idea of the scope or nature of their activities until the trouble came [5]. The result of the interaction of these factors with a credit market downturn — in the SIVs and elsewhere — is the most sustained period of instability in U.S. financial markets in many years.

What Makes a Financial Crisis?

Since August 2007, the Federal Reserve has recognized deteriorating financial markets as a principal threat to the economic outlook. Despite soaring commodity prices and a falling dollar, which would normally raise inflation fears, the Fed has eased monetary policy, reducing its target for the federal funds rate from 5.25% (the level that was established in June of 2006) to 2.25%. It has declared its willingness to provide liquidity to the financial system [6]. In the process of reaching the lower interest rate target, the Fed, in its open market operations, buys securities from depository institutions, giving them new cash to lend. Lower rates themselves, of course, stimulate demand for credit, as more investment projects become potentially profitable once they can be funded at lower cost.

In recent years, such actions appeared to be sufficient to prevent financial shocks from developing into crises. Neither the stock market crash of 1987 (where the stock market lost 23% of its value in one day), the near collapse of the Long-Term Capital Management hedge fund in 1998 (which threatened to paralyze the bond markets), the "dot.com" crash in 2000-200 1 (which again erased trillions of dollars in stock value), nor the September 2001 terrorist attacks (which closed markets and disrupted payment systems) was followed by the kind of prolonged financial stress observed in late 2007 and into 2008.

Many observers believe it is premature to speak of a financial "crisis" at this point, when relatively few financial firms have actually failed and when the economy continues to grow, albeit at a slower pace. Tight credit conditions, in this view, simply reflect a normal market cycle: after a period of financial expansion driven by low interest rates, abundant credit, and a relaxed attitude towards risk, there inevitably comes a correction: losses occur, forcing lenders to raise new capital or make fewer loans to rebuild their capital and reserves. According to this line of argument, the process is self-correcting, and given that most financial institutions entered the current period of turbulence with large reserves of capital to cushion against losses, should be allowed to play out.

Treasury Secretary Paulson, for example, stated in January 2008 that large losses reported by several major institutions were a sign that the system is working: "As markets reassess, we should not be surprised or disappointed to see financial institutions writing down assets and strengthening balance sheets. This is market discipline in action and should enhance market confidence over time" [7].

While the self-correcting properties of markets are generally acknowledged, several analysts identify forces that work in the other direction. In their models, shocks produce other shocks, multiplying the effects of an original loss.

In a recent paper, Greenlaw et al. focus on the pro-cyclical nature of leverage [8]. They assume that firms prefer to maintain a more or less constant level of leverage, or ratio of total assets to capital. As the assets that make up a firm's capital base gain in value, the firm can support more assets on the balance sheet. Balance sheet expansion, in turn, involves asset purchases, boosting asset prices further.

When prices are falling, however, the cycle works in reverse. As its capital loses value, the firm must shrink its balance sheet to maintain a given leverage ratio. As firms sell assets to reduce balance sheet exposure, asset prices are driven down. Because financial firms are typically highly leveraged, a balance sheet adjustment of any given size is multiplied. The authors assume that commercial banks have leverage ratios of about 10:1, meaning that a $1 billion capital loss requires a $10 billion reduction in their portfolio of assets, which consists primarily of loans. In other words, price shocks to a firm cause behavior that reinforces the movement of prices. These self-reinforcing cycles are illustrated in Figure 3.

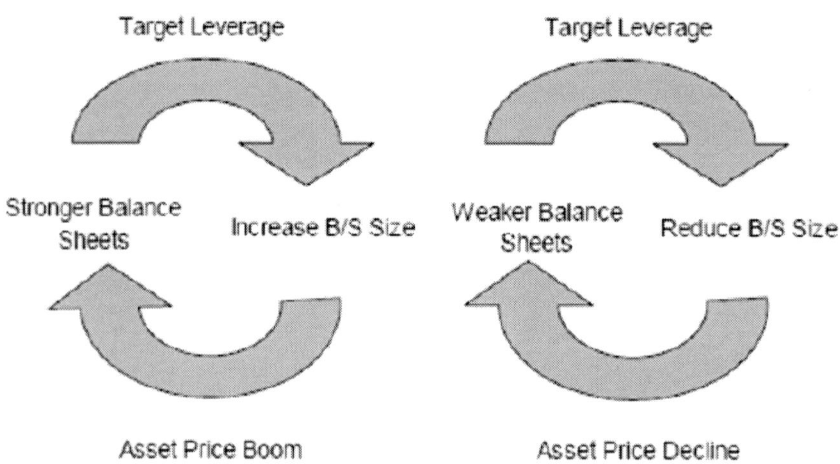

Source: David Greenlaw, Jan Hatzius, Anil Kashyap, and Hyun Song Shin, "Leveraged Losses: Lessons from the Mortgage Meltdown," U.S. Monetary Forum Conference Draft, Feb. 29, 2008, p. 30.

Figure 3. The Leverage Cycle.

In a 1996 paper, Bernanke, Gertler, and Gilchrist also seek a solution to the "longstanding puzzle" that large fluctuations in aggregate economic activity sometimes arise from what appear to be relatively small impulses" [9]. They describe a mechanism they call the "financial accelerator." They argue that the cost of external finance to a firm — its cost of borrowing — is inversely related to its net worth. A fall in asset prices reduces the collateral value of the firm's assets, which hinders or raises the cost of borrowing. By simultaneously increasing the need for external finance and restricting its availability, a negative shock causes the firm to reduce spending and production. "To the extent that negative shocks to the economy reduce the net worth of borrowers..., the spending and production effects of the initial shock will be amplified" [10].

These two models describe similar effects, acting upon both the supply of and demand for credit. The models suggest that shocks to financial firms can have disproportionate impacts on real economic activity. When financial turbulence interacts with expectations of a contraction in real economic activity, the prospect of another negative spiral emerges. Martin Feldstein, chairman of the Council of Economic Advisers under President Reagan, describes the situation as a kind of Catch-22: "The credit flows needed for economic expansion require confidence in the values of financial assets, but market participants may not have such confidence while the risk of recession hangs over us" [11].

Federal Reserve Governor Frederic Mishkin elaborated on this theme in November 2007:

> The second type of risk that I consider central to the understanding of financial stability is what I call *macroeconomic risk* — that is, an increase in the probability that a financial disruption will cause significant deterioration in the real economy. Because economic downturns typically result in even greater uncertainty about asset values, such episodes may involve an adverse feedback loop whereby financial disruptions cause investment and consumer spending to decline, which, in turn, causes economic activity to contract. Such contraction then increases uncertainty about the value of assets, and, as a result, the financial disruption worsens. In turn, this development causes economic activity to contract further in a perverse cycle [12].

This scenario, according to Mishkin, explains why the Federal Reserve is unwilling to assume that markets will self-correct without serious damage to the real economy. Financial instability, "if allowed to develop fully," could have severely negative consequences in both financial markets and the global economy [13]. To address the risk — however small — that the current situation could develop into a full-blown financial crisis, cutting off credit flows that support investment and spending, the Fed (and other central banks and regulators) have taken extraordinary steps. In one description that is perhaps not entirely hyperbolic, central bankers have decided to "tear up their rule books and established practices...to inject cash, resuscitate the interbank market, and hopefully ease the credit squeeze" [14].

Government Interventions Open Market Operations and Monetary Policy

The Fed has made aggressive use of its monetary policy tools: cutting the federal funds rate target six times, including dramatic cuts of 75 basis points (0.75%) in January and March of 2008, and using its open market operations to inject liquidity into the banking system. Early cuts appeared aimed specifically at financial markets, but more recently, as the Fed has explicitly recognized that market conditions have become a drag on real economic activity, the distinction between actions aimed at restoring financial stability and those aimed at macroeconomic stimulus has become blurred, if it exists at all.

The Discount Window

In addition to open market operations, the Fed can provide liquidity by lending to individual banks through its discount window. Eligible banks can borrow short- term (usually overnight) directly from the central bank. Whereas open market operations target the system as a whole, discount lending provides support to particular banks with a need for liquidity. Another distinction is that discount widow borrowings can be collateralized using a broader range of assets that can open market transactions, where the only acceptable collateral is U.S. Treasury or agency securities [15].

On August 10, 2007, in its first public response to worsening financial conditions, the Fed announced a 50 basis point cut in the discount rate. (The Federal Funds rate was not cut until the next regularly-scheduled meeting of the Federal Open Market Committee in September 2007)

A limitation of discount lending is that banks do not like to use it. Borrowing at the discount window may send a signal to the markets that a bank has liquidity problems. In an environment like that of late 2007, when interbank lending was already constrained by credit risk fears, the perceived costs of such a perception of financial weakness rise. To overcome the "stigma" of the discount window, the Fed introduced a new method for providing liquidity, the Term Auction Facility.

On March 11, 2008, the Fed took a highly unusual step: it expanded access to the discount window to primary dealers in U.S. Treasury securities. The primary dealers are large securities firms, like Merrill Lynch and Morgan Stanley, which the Fed does not regulate.

Term Auction Facility (TAF)

Despite the Fed's efforts to restore liquidity using its standard tools, markets continued to be tight. In December 2007, the Fed, together with the central banks of Canada, Britain, the European Union, and Switzerland, announced "measures designed to address elevated pressures in short-term funding markets" [16].

The Term Auction Facility (TAF) has conducted a series of auctions of short-term loan funds to banks, accepting as collateral the same wide variety of assets that can be used to secure discount window borrowing. Auctions involve a fixed amount of funds, at a rate to be determined by competitive bidding. Since December, the TAF has held two auctions per month, and about 60 to 75 financial institutions have submitted bids at each. TAF funds are loaned for periods of 28 to 35 days. The amount of funds provided to the bidding banks was $40 billion in December, $60 billion in both January and February, with $100 billion projected for March. The total — $260 billion — thus will exceed by a considerable margin the economic stimulus package (P.L. 110-185) passed by Congress in February 2008, which will provide about $160 billion in tax rebates and reductions.

The TAF program — and efforts to restore liquidity to the banking system generally — raise certain questions. If the current financial situation is fundamentally a reaction to a period of too-easy access to credit and of excess liquidity, is providing more liquidity the appropriate response? If market discipline operates by forcing banks to absorb losses and shrink their balance sheets, do the Fed's actions to expand credit prolong the adjustment process? Provision of liquidity lowers interest rates, which is good for borrowers and for interest-sensitive economic sectors such as housing, but not for savers, because rates of return on conservative investments like bank CDs and money market funds are depressed. It could be argued that the Fed appears to be rescuing those who caused the problem at the expense of others who had nothing to do with it.

Others question the efficacy of the mechanism: supplying liquidity to banks does not automatically translate into more lending [17]. If elevated credit risk concerns are what is causing tight credit markets, liquidity provision may be the equivalent of "pushing on a string."

In addition, the Fed is aware that actions that appear to undercut market discipline may encourage excessive risk-taking in the future. But the risk that financial market problems may cause or exacerbate a slowdown in macroeconomic growth outweighs all other factors, even though there is as yet no indisputable evidence of such a link. The risks of waiting until there is such evidence are not acceptable to the Fed. Liquidity provision is the principal tool available to the Fed, and its recent actions suggest that it will continue to use it.

On February 27, 2008, in his semiannual monetary report to the Congress, Fed Chairman Bernanke testified that the TAF, in conjunction with the parallel programs of other central banks, "appear[s] to have contributed to some improvement in short- term funding markets" [18]. On March 7, however, the Fed — citing "heightened liquidity pressures in term funding markets" [19] — increased the amount of funds for the two TAF auctions planned for the month of March (from $30 billion to $50 billion each) and announced that it would conduct a series of repurchase transactions expected to provide another $100 billion into the banking system [20].

Treasury's "Super-SIV" Proposal

In the fall of 2007, when public attention focused on SIVs that were suddenly unable to find buyers for asset-backed commercial paper, a number of large banks met with Treasury officials and designed a financial structure to alleviate SIV funding problems. They proposed that a consortium of private banks create a "Master Liquidity Enhancement Conduit" (MLEC), to be capitalized entirely by the banks, which would buy assets from existing SIVs and fund these purchases in exactly the same way that the SIVs had done in the past: by issuing short-term commercial paper. The expectation was that commercial paper issued by the MLEC would be viewed as safe because of the vast financial resources of the participating banks and because the Treasury had endorsed the plan (although MLEC's debt would not carry any formal government guarantee).

The MLEC concept was announced on October 15, 2007, in a joint press release from J.P. Morgan Chase, Bank of America, and Citigroup, which noted that the Treasury had facilitated the agreement [21]. (The Federal Reserve had no comment on the plan, then or later.) Negotiations proceeded over the following weeks and months, but although press reports suggested that agreement was near, in the end banks were unwilling to commit capital to the project. The apparent coup-de-grace was delivered on December 20, 2007, when the three largest Japanese banks declined to participate [22]. A few days later, the effort to launch the MLEC was abandoned.

There are two explanations for the failure of the MLEC proposal. First, it was not clear that the concept was economically viable. The underlying problem was that the mortgage-backed assets held by SIVs had lost value and might continue to lose value unless the housing market recovered. How would transferring those assets (and losses) to a "super-SIV" help? The assumption behind the MLEC proposal was that markets were in a state of panic and that prices of mortgage-backed assets at that time were below their fundamental values. If liquidity could be restored, the super-SIV could simply hold assets until markets stabilized and rational valuations returned, and make a profit. Meanwhile, the MLEC would have given the SIVs a better price than they could have found elsewhere, allowing the sponsoring banks and other investors to cap their losses, and avoiding a "fire sale" by desperate SIVs at the brink of insolvency, which would have driven values even lower, exacerbating the general financial situation and further roiling housing markets.

In retrospect, it appears that prospective MLEC participants found this assumption and scenario less persuasive than an alternative view: that mortgage assets were not necessarily priced below fundamental values, but might still have some distance to fall. In this analysis, the SIVs' problem was not one of liquidity, but of solvency, and the notion that they could be rescued at a profit was deemed to be unrealistic.

Second, as time went on, it became apparent that the SIVs did not in fact pose an acute threat to their sponsoring banks. By the end of 2007, over $109 billion in SIV assets had been brought back onto the sponsoring banks' balance sheets, without triggering a solvency crisis in those banks [23]. SIV assets became simply one of many sources of financial pain.

With hindsight, the SIV issue may have been overstated in the fall of 2007. It was a serious problem, and contributed to perceptions of elevated credit and valuation risk that fed the general financial turmoil, but it was not the key to the entire systemic disturbance. Rather, SIVs were one of several trouble spots that may be more properly characterized as symptoms of an underlying problem, or set of problems.

Provision of New Capital to Financial Institutions

As noted above, when banks and other financial institutions suffer declines in the value of their capital, to maintain constant leverage ratios they must either shrink their balance sheets or raise new capital. From a regulatory perspective, the latter method is usually preferable, since it does not require that new lending be curtailed. For the government to bail out troubled financial institutions through an injection of public funds is rare, although many assume that certain large institutions are "too big to fail" — that is, that the failure of such an institution could have adverse systemic consequences so severe that the government would have no choice but to intervene. The Treasury and the Federal Reserve officially deny that any such policy exists, because the moral hazard issue — which (as discussed above) may be a secondary effect of the Fed's liquidity support programs — is very clear here. If institutions believe they will be rescued from insolvency, they will take imprudent risks: the calculus becomes "Heads, I win; tails, the taxpayers lose."

Although several major financial institutions experienced severe financial stress in 2007, there were no reports that the U.S. government was preparing to step in to prevent a spectacular collapse. In fact, troubled U.S. institutions were able to raise significant amounts of new capital. Much of this money — over $30 billion by one estimate [24] — has come from government sources, but not the American government. Instead, sovereign wealth funds operated by China, Singapore, Abu Dhabi, and other countries have taken large equity stakes in Citigroup, Merrill Lynch, Morgan Stanley, and other firms, including leading European financial institutions.

While some find sovereign wealth fund investment to be problematic [25] and are uneasy at the prospect of foreign ownership of substantial shares of key Western financial institutions, there is little doubt that such investment has eased the adjustment process for the recipients and mitigated the systemic (and perhaps macroeconomic) impact of market turmoil. It is not known whether U.S. government officials played a role in soliciting these capital contributions.

On Thursday, March 13, 2008, it became known that the Federal Reserve had extended credit to Bear Stearns, a large investment bank whose liquidity problems had driven it to the brink of collapse. As market perceptions of Bear Stearns' weakness grew, it became unable to borrow and its customers sought to retrieve their invested funds. The Fed was unwilling to allow the firm to collapse, since a liquidation would have meant the dumping of billions of dollars in mortgage-backed and other securities on the market, at a time when demand was low. The resulting fall in prices would have exacerbated the balance sheet problems of other institutions, perhaps triggering further collapses.

Over the weekend, the Fed worked with J.P. Morgan Chase to work out an agreement by which Morgan would acquire Bear. In order for the deal to proceed, the Fed had to accept Bear's "less liquid assets" as collateral for $30 billion in loans. The final sale price was $2 per share: a remarkable plunge from the end of 2007, when Bear's financial statements reported a book value of $80 per share, and from January 2007, when the shares traded at a high of $172.61.

In the wake of the Bear Stearns rescue, the Fed has been criticized for widening the financial "safety net" to include a firm that was neither insured by the Federal Deposit Insurance Corporation nor subject to the oversight of the Fed or any other banking agency. Bear Stearns was widely considered to have been among the most aggressive and reckless speculators in the subprime market.

POLICY ISSUES: ARE REGULATORS' TOOLS ADEQUATE?

This prolonged period of financial stress raises questions about the ability of regulators to monitor, prevent, or respond to market instability. Policy makers may consider a number of approaches.

Information

First, some observers believe that regulators lack comprehensive information about large areas of the markets. No federal agency has direct supervisory authority over hedge funds, nonbank lenders, over-the-counter derivatives trading, private equity funds, all of which demand liquidity and can become the trigger for systemic instability. When regulated firms create off-balance sheet entities, oversight becomes more difficult. According to Secretary Paulson, "regulators didn't have clear enough visibility with what was going on in terms of these off-balance-sheet SIVs" [26]. Banking and securities laws could be amended to authorize regulators to require more disclosure and reporting from (1) currently unregulated firms and sectors and (2) about off-the-books activities of regulated firms.

U.S. financial regulation is divided among agencies specializing in single markets: futures, individual banking sectors, or securities. In today's markets, however, firms' activities regularly cross those lines. An integrated firm like Merrill Lynch or Citigroup files reports with half a dozen agencies — would a single, consolidated supervisor be better able to interpret this information and assess market conditions?

Others question whether regulators can be expected to monitor overall market conditions, when the current turmoil suggests that even market participants lack that capacity. The invention of new and complex derivative instruments and securities has been a major profit center in the financial industry for several decades. In other words, while transparency benefits regulators and public investors, opacity can be a source of income for market intermediaries and professional traders. The problem of hard-to-value assets and unverifiable trading models is likely to persist.

Another view is that regulators had plenty of information indicating that trouble was imminent, but failed to take adequate preventive measures. According to Martin Feldstein, even though "the Fed's examiners have complete access to all of the transactions of the banks that they supervise [and] can also examine indirectly what nonbank financial institutions are doing," the Fed failed to provide appropriate supervisory oversight for major money center banks, making such technical errors as understating liabilities associated with off-balance sheet activities and overstating the quality of bank asset values that were the result of the housing bubble [27]. There is a natural tendency for regulators to share industry's enthusiasm for the latest financial innovation or strategy, as long as it is generating profits that enable banks to meet capital requirements and maintain healthy levels of reserves. It is difficult, as Alan Greenspan put it, to be the one who takes away the punch bowl when the party is just getting started [28]. Federal bank agencies addressed securitization and off- balance sheet finance more than a decade ago, but characterized them as useful risk management tools [29]. (Which, in normal times, they are).

Speculation

Financial speculation presents another set of policy choices. In general, speculation is a benign and useful activity: speculators provide liquidity and help markets allocate resources efficiently. The current episode, however, illustrates that speculative excesses and errors can cause liquidity to dry up and disrupt markets.

Successful speculation rewards risk-taking. Recent developments in finance make it possible to unbundle the risks embedded in traditional financial instruments. A mortgage, for example, carries credit risk, interest rate risk, and prepayment risk, but with derivatives and CDOs, each of these risks can be disaggregated and made the basis of a financial bet. Increasingly, speculators identify financial propositions with a high probability of making a small profit, and a very small chance of a large loss. The SIV model, for example, captured the spread between short-term and longterm rates, earning a modest return that was almost risk-free unless there were to be a major disruption in the commercial paper market, which was normally very large and liquid. The CDO market relies on the narrow spread between what homebuyers pay and what investors will pay for the identical mortgages repackaged. Using derivatives, it is possible to construct similar trades based on tiny variations in observed historical relationships among a multitude of economic variables.

Of course, a strategy that promises a small but seemingly predictable return does not appeal to most investment bankers: Treasury bills offer the same risk/reward characteristics. What the bankers do is add leverage: if they borrow a high multiple of their own capital and put those funds into the same trading position, the returns to their own capital are magnified. Of course, the potential losses are magnified to exactly the same degree. Then why is leveraged speculation attractive?

One answer, put forward by Raghuram Rajan, former chief economist of the International Monetary Fund, is that compensation structures reward short-term performance and ignore long-term risk [30]. That a strategy is likely to fail spectacularly every ten or twenty years is not a disincentive to the leveraged trader: he will probably receive several large annual bonuses before the bad year comes, and even then may keep his job, since many of his peers will probably have incurred similar losses. The CEO of Morgan Stanley, for example, received no bonus for 2007, but kept the $40 million from the year before [31].

The combination of modern financial engineering and short-term incentives may distort or weaken market discipline and lead to excessive risk-taking. The costs of failed speculation are not always borne by the speculators themselves but may be widely distributed throughout the financial system and, in extreme cases, may fall upon the economy as a whole. Is there a case for more stringent regulation to restrain speculation or limit the potential damage from speculative losses?

Financial supervisors can impose higher capital and reserve requirements on regulated firms, and can control the amount of leverage such firms extend to their unregulated customers. Such controls would smooth out the peaks and troughs of financial industry returns: this would mean, in effect, putting a brake on periods of economic and financial expansion. Rajan suggests that significant portions of bankers' pay could be held in escrow for long periods, and that losses be factored in before final disbursement [32]. The degree of support for initiatives such as these among regulators and policy makers is likely to depend on how the current financial turmoil is resolved, and at what cost.

REFERENCES

[1] Brian Caplen, "Credit Suisse CEO: Clear View Curtails Crisis Fallout," *The Banker*, January 1, 2008.

[2] Risky bank loans equivalent to high-yield "junk" bonds, often made in support of corporate takeovers or buyouts.

[3] Commercial paper is used as a source of short-term borrowing by many firms, financial and nonfinancial. The maturity is generally between three months and one year.

[4] Adrian Blundell-Wignall, Structured Products: Implications for Financial Markets, *[OECD] Financial Market Trends*, No. 93, 2007, p. 45.

[5] For example, Citigroup' s SIVs held about $100 billion in assets at the peak, yet the firm's quarterly report to the Securities and Exchange Commission for the second quarter of 2007 contained no reference to them. (The third quarter report, of course, devoted considerable space to the associated problems and potential losses.)

[6] Liquidity, in central banking terms, means maintaining the flow of credit. The Fed's declarations signal market participants not to allow credit decisions to be governed by fears that the opposite party may have temporary cash flow problems.

[7] Martin Crutsinger, "Paulson: No Simple Solution to Housing Crisis," *York Dispatch*, January 7, 2008.

[8] David Greenlaw, Jan Hatzius, Anil Kashyap, and Hyun Song Shin, "Leveraged Losses: Lessons from the Mortgage Meltdown," U.S. Monetary Forum Conference Draft, February 29, 2008, 47 p.

[9] Ben Bernanke, Mark Gertler, and Simon Gilchrist, "The Financial Accelerator and the Flight to Quality," Review of Economics and Statistics, vol. 78, February 1996, p. 1.

[10] Ibid., p. 2.

[11] Martin Feldstein, "Our Economic Dilemma," *Wall Street Journal*, February 20, 2008, p. A15.

[12] Frederic S . Mishkin, "Financial Instability and Monetary Policy," Speech at the Risk USA 2007 Conference, New York, November 5, 2007.

[13] Ibid.

[14] "Central Banks' Action Is Welcome But Long-Term Rethink Is Needed," *The Banker*, January 1, 2008.

[15] Agency bonds are those issued by government-sponsored enterprises like Fannie Mae and Freddie Mac.

[16] "Federal Reserve Actions," Press Release, December 12, 2007.

[17] See, e.g., Steven Sloan, "Fed Pushes Harder, But Sentiment Isn't Shifting," *American Banker*, vol. 178, March 10, 2008, p. 1.

[18] "Semiannual Monetary Policy Report to the Congress," before the House Committee on Financial Services, February 27, 2008. (Identical testimony was presented before the Senate Committee on Banking, Housing, and Urban Affairs on February 28.)

[19] See [http://www.federalreserve.gov/newsevents/press/monetary/20080307a.htm].

[20] A repurchase agreement is a securities transaction that is equivalent to a loan. One party (the Fed, in this case) "buys" a security from another, who promises to buy it back later at a higher price. The difference between the prices is equivalent to interest; the security itself serves as collateral.

[21] "Global Banks Announce Plans for Major Liquidity Facility to Bolster Asset-Backed Commercial Paper Markets," *PR Newswire*, October 5, 2007.

[22] Atsuko Fukase, "Japanese Banks Balk at Aiding SIV Fund," *Wall Street Journal*, December 20, 2007, p. C9.

[23] The exact total is unknown. The $109 billion figure represents announced transactions by five banks: Citigroup ($49 billion), HSBC ($45 billion), Rabobank ($7.6 billion), Societe General ($4.3 billion), and Standard Chartered ($3 billion). See "Bringing It All Back Home," *American Banker*, vol. 172, December 17, 2007, p. 1.

[24] Gillian Tett, "Sovereign funds face growing US pressure to address market fears," *Financial Times*, January 24, 2008, p. 1.

[25] See CRS Report RL34336, *Sovereign Wealth Funds: Background and Policy Issues for Congress*, by Martin A. Weiss.

[26] Carrick Mollenkamp, Deborah Solomon and Craig Karmin, "Call to Brave for $100 Billion Rescue; Banks Seek Investors For Fund to Shore Up Commercial Paper," *Wall Street Journal*, October 16, 2007, p. C1.

[27] Martin Feldstein, "Our Economic Dilemma," *Wall Street Journal*, February 20, 2008, p. A15.

[28] According to some sources, he was quoting his predecessor, Chairman William McChesney Martin, Jr. The remark is attributed to every Fed chairman sooner or later.

[29] See, e.g., Office of the Comptroller of the Currency, "Interest Rate Risk Management: Questions and Answers," OCC 95-28, June 20, 1995, at [http://www.occ.treas.gov/ftp/ bulletin/95-28.txt].

[30] Raghuram Rajan, "Bankers' Pay is Deeply Flawed," *Financial Times*, January 9, 2008, p. 11.

[31] The firm wrote down the value of its assets by $9.4 billion in the last quarter of 2007, but increased its year-end bonus pool by 18%.

[32] Ibid.

In: Financial Crisis in America ISBN 978-1-60692-191-3
Editor: Raymond T. Ovanhouser, pp.97-121 © 2009 Nova Science Publishers, Inc.

Chapter 4

WOULD A HOUSING CRASH CAUSE A RECESSION?*

Marc Labonte

ABSTRACT

After years of rapid appreciation, house prices barely rose in the second quarter of 2007, and many analysts expect price declines in many markets in the near future. There have already been large drops in house sales and residential investment (house building). Given the central role that the housing boom has played in the current economic expansion, many observers fear that a crash in the housing market will lead to an economy-wide recession. They are concerned that a fall in house prices could spill over into a decline in aggregate spending through four channels.

First, builders could respond to lower prices by reducing residential investment, an important component of gross domestic product (GDP). Second, since mortgages are backed by the value of the underlying house, a fall in prices could feed through to financial instability. Both of these effects have already been felt, with the rate of residential investment falling by double digits since mid-2006, and the entire financial sector undergoing a liquidity crunch triggered by problems with subprime mortgage-backed securities in August 2007.

Third, a fall in housing prices could lead to a decline in consumer spending through a negative "wealth effect." Some economists have argued that when house prices were rising, households responded to their greater

---

* Excerpted from CRS Report RL34244 dated November 7, 2007.

housing wealth by increasing their consumption spending; were prices to fall, presumably the effect would be reversed. This effect is difficult to measure and faces some theoretical objections. For example, every housing transaction is composed of a buyer and seller. When house prices fall, sellers are made poorer but buyers are made wealthier, in the sense that they can now devote less of their income to mortgage payments and more to other consumption.

Fourth, the impending reset of mortgages to higher payments for many recent buyers could lead to a significant increase in the share of households suffering from financial distress. For some homeowners, a fall in prices would eliminate the option to refinance to avoid the distress. These homeowners may then be forced to reduce consumption spending in response.

Economic growth could decline in response to falling house prices through any of these four channels if all else remained equal. But it is possible that spending in other parts of the economy could rise and pick up the slack. And the government is not a neutral bystander when it comes to the path of aggregate spending. It can use expansionary fiscal or monetary policy to offset decreases to aggregate spending. The Federal Reserve has already responded to the housing and financial downturn by reducing short-term interest rates.

Most economic models suggest that a fall in prices in the range that has been predicted would not be enough to single-handedly cause a recession. But some observers think it may be enough to tip an already tepid economy into recession.

INTRODUCTION

After several years of unprecedented price appreciation, the housing boom has come to an end, and some economists believe that prices in many markets will experience a near-term decline. The housing boom has gripped the public's imagination in the current economic expansion, and many observers now wonder if a housing crash would cause an economic recession (a sustained period of sub-par economic growth and higher unemployment). This chapter will examine the channels through which changes in the housing market affect the economy, and what policy options might be used to offset its adverse effects. It will begin with a brief discussion of the housing boom and its aftermath.

THE HOUSING BOOM AND ITS AFTERMATH

Figure 1 illustrates the unprecedented rates of increase in house prices that have occurred in recent years as measured by the Office of Federal Housing Enterprise Oversight's house price index. As Figure 1 shows, while appreciation rates have fallen significantly since 2005, house prices are not yet falling by this measure. Price appreciation ground to a halt in the second quarter of 2007, however, and other data sources show small decreases in house prices over the past year. Although one quarter of zero price appreciation does not make for a trend, many analysts believe that house prices will fall significantly in the next few years.

Most parts of the country have seen the same pattern of boom and bust, although the timing has differed. Rapid appreciation rates began in California and the Northeast between 2000 and 2002, moved to the Mid-Atlantic, Hawaii, Florida, and Nevada by 2004, and the Southwest, Mountain region, and Pacific Northwest by 2005. The only regions of the country that did not experience an extraordinary housing boom in this decade were the Midwest and South. Prices increased more than 90% in five years in Florida, California, Arizona, Nevada, Rhode Island, Maryland, Hawaii, and the District of Columbia. Prices in the first five of these states fell through the first half of 2007.

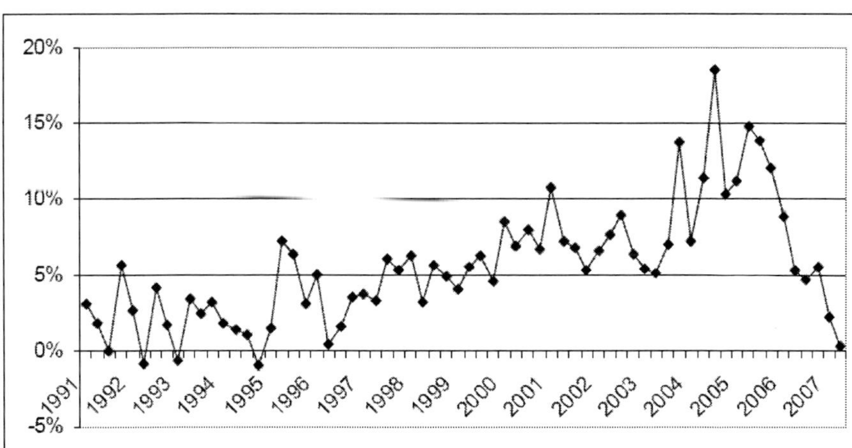

Source: Office of Housing Enterprise Oversight.

Notes: The house price index measures the change in price of repeat-sale, single-family, owner-occupied homes. The changes are not adjusted for general price inflation.

Figure 1. Quarterly Changes in House Price Index (Annualized Rate).

The proximate reason that rapid price appreciation abruptly came to an end — and why analysts believe prices will continue to deteriorate — was a sharp fall in housing sales. During the boom, sales rose to very high levels. Existing home sales fell by 8% in 2006 and 13% in the 12 months ending in August 2007. New home sales fell by 18% in 2006 and 21% in the 12 months ending in August 2007. One reason that some analysts argue house prices will continue to fall is because the number of unsold houses on the market has risen sharply. For example, it is estimated that there was 10 months supply of existing houses on the market in August 2007, up from 4 months supply in 2004.

Lower appreciation rates have already had a profound effect on residential investment (house building). Housing starts fell by 13% in 2006 and 25% in the 12 months ending in August 2007. Residential investment has fallen by 16% in the last four quarters. Residential investment is a component of gross domestic product (GDP) — if it falls, then GDP falls, all else equal.

A housing crash could be defined as a fall in residential investment or a fall in house prices. In the former case, a crash has already occurred. In the latter case, it has not yet occurred nationally, although it may be starting to occur in some local markets.

Boom or Bubble?

To determine why the housing boom ended and how far house prices might fall in the future, if at all, a key question to answer is to what extent the boom was caused by an asset bubble. An asset bubble refers to a rise in price that is due to "irrational exuberance" rather than changes in economic fundamentals [1]. Unfortunately, it is difficult to identify bubbles until after the fact since economic models are based on assumptions that individuals behave rationally. If individuals always acted rationally, a bubble, by definition, could not exist since individuals would anticipate future price declines and reduce their demand for housing, thereby preventing a bubble from forming before it had started.

Rapidly rising prices do not, by themselves, prove that there is a bubble. In fact, there were many changes in economic fundamentals that, by making housing more affordable, increased the demand for housing over this period. Average after-tax income was rising, and, most importantly, mortgage rates fell from 8% in 2000 to less than 6% in 2003. Lower mortgage rates significantly reduce the cost of financing a home purchase, and would thereby increase the demand for housing. With housing supply unable to adjust immediately, increased demand would lead to some rise in real prices (beyond general price inflation). Yet mortgage rates did not fall any further after 2003, and the boom nevertheless continued in some parts of the country until 2006. Clearly, some other factor must be responsible for the later years of the boom.

To make mortgages more affordable, more borrowers took out adjustable rate mortgages (ARMs), which allowed them to reduce their initial mortgage rates below the fixed rate by taking on interest rate risk [2]. Affordability also improved, at least temporarily, thanks to the rise in alternative mortgages in the current boom, and this increased demand. Broadly defined, alternative mortgages are those that do not follow the traditional fixed payment structure. Alternative mortgages and smaller down payments expanded credit to buyers who could not previously borrow and temporarily lowered borrowing costs [3]. Borrowing costs were lowered through mortgage products such as "interest only" loans that allowed borrowers to make no payment on the mortgage principal for an introductory period. The rise in alternative mortgages could be seen as a change in economic fundamentals that caused the boom, or it could be seen as a symptom of the bubble. In the latter view, buyers took on mortgages that they could not afford or did not understand because they believed that prices would continue to rise.

Although the boom may have been initially driven by greater affordability as a result of rising incomes and lower borrowing costs, unsurprisingly rising prices led to a rapid deterioration in affordability from 2003 on, until ultimately the boom ended. In 2006, housing was less affordable than at any point in the previous 20 years, according to the housing affordability index, shown in Figure 2. Unlike the deterioration in affordability during the 1 970s and 1 980s, which was driven primarily by higher mortgage rates, the recent deterioration was driven primarily by higher house prices.

In most markets, an increase in demand would be expected to have little lasting effect on price because producers can increase supply in response to higher demand relatively quickly, causing prices to return to their previous level. Housing markets are different because it takes longer to add to the housing supply and because some areas have land constraints. In areas with land constraints, rising prices are not necessarily proof that a bubble is forming. And because of the lag in supply, a pattern of rising followed by falling house prices (as new supply becomes available) could be consistent with economic fundamentals, and does not constitute conclusive evidence that a bubble has occurred.

Whether the boom was a bubble is arguably academic at this point, since the end of the boom will affect the economy in either case. Nevertheless, it is an important question moving forward because of what it implies for the future. If the housing market is currently experiencing a bursting bubble, then prices may fall farther in the future than if the rise in prices were a reflection of economic fundamentals.

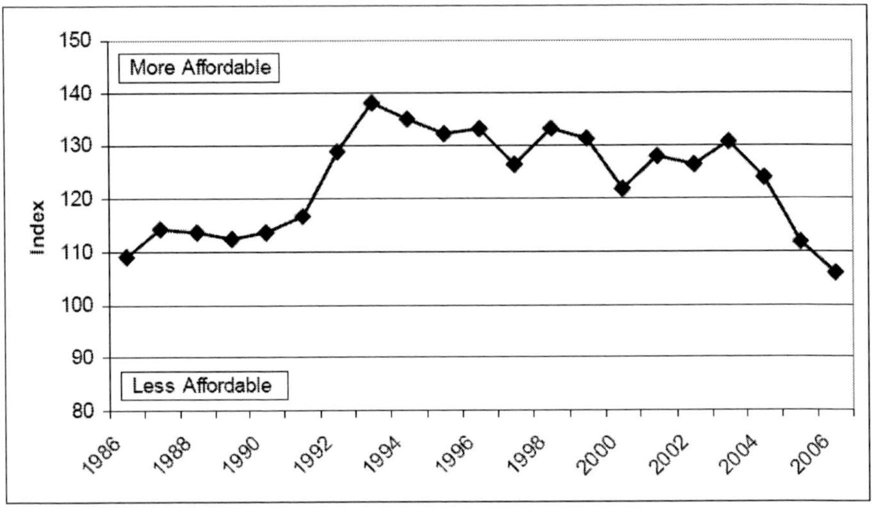

Source: National Association of Realtors.

Notes: Affordability index is based on median house prices, median family income, and mortgage rates, using a composite of fixed and adjustable mortgage rates. The index defines higher values as more affordable.

Figure 2. Housing Affordability Index, 1986-2006.

A bursting bubble may also magnify the economic effects of a housing downturn since it would represent an independent shock to the economy. A bubble could deflate slowly via a long period of stagnant prices or suddenly. It is the latter scenario that threatens macroeconomic stability since the economy has proven resilient to gradual adjustments. Indeed, stagnant housing prices have not derailed the expansion to date.

Macroeconomic Effects of a Housing Crash

Although changes in house prices have no direct effect on GDP (since GDP measures current production in constant dollars), there are several channels through which the economy could be affected by a housing crash. Lower housing prices could lead to a slowdown in house building, to problems in the wider financial system, a reduction in housing wealth could lead to a reduction in consumption spending, and cause household debt burdens to become unsustainable. Each effect is discussed below.

Effects on the Housing Industry

Residential investment (house building) would respond directly to lower house prices. Holding construction costs constant, lower housing prices would lead to lower revenues and profits for the housing industry. As a result, fewer new houses would be built, reducing the residential investment component of GDP. Besides construction, related industries such as real estate services and home improvement services are likely to be negatively affected by a housing bust. Building projects are lengthy to complete, so residential investment is also sensitive to future prices — if builders believe that prices will fall, due to falling income, rising mortgage rates, or a deflating bubble, some will forgo new projects now. This may explain why residential investment has already declined sharply although prices are not yet falling nationally.

Because of its sensitivity to changes in interest rates and prices, the residential investment sector has historically been one of the more volatile sectors of the economy, as shown in Figure 3. During the housing boom, it was one of the fastest growing sectors of the economy, growing an average of 9% annually in 2003-2005. In 2005, The Economist estimated that "over two-fifths of all private-sector jobs created since 2001 have been in housing-related sectors, such as construction, real estate, and mortgage brokering"[4]. Beginning in the fourth quarter of 2005, residential investment stopped increasing. Since the second quarter of 2006, it has declined by more than 10% a quarter at annualized rates. Over this period, residential investment has reduced GDP growth by an average of 1.0 percentage points, all else equal [5]. Surprisingly, construction employment has fallen by only 1% so far, in part because commercial construction has remained strong.

The recent contraction in residential investment is not the first. There were two similar episodes at the beginning and end of the 1980s. Both of these episodes, as well as the current one, coincided with contractionary monetary policy (periods of rising short-term interest rates). From 1980 to 1982, residential investment shrank by a cumulative 40.6% in real terms, while GDP grew by 0.2%. From 1988 to 1991, residential investment shrank by 23.9%, while GDP grew by 9.2%. It is useful to note that the latter bust preceded the recession, which did not begin until July 1990. The period of monetary tightening preceding that recession spanned from 1988 to 1989.

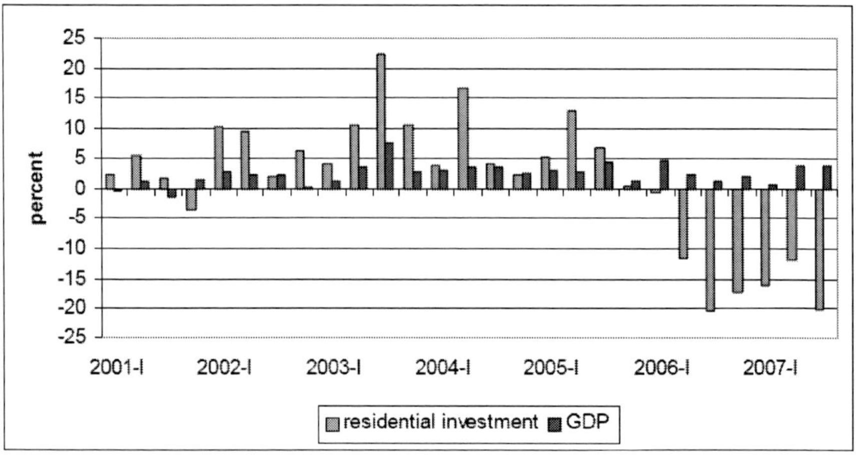

Source: Bureau of Economic Analysis.
Notes: Quarterly growth rates have been annualized. Data are adjusted for inflation.

Figure 3. Quarterly Growth Rate of Residential Investment and GDP, 2001-2007.

The current housing bust has not yet bottomed out, but the decline in residential investment was already as large as the 1988-1991 episode by the third quarter of 2007.

Table 1. Historical Declines in Residential Investment

	Change in Residential Investment	GDP Growth	Federal Funds Rate
1980-1982	-40.6%	0.2%	Rose from 9.0% in 7/80 to 19.1% in 6/81
1988-1991	-23.9%	9.2%	Rose from 6.6% in 2/88 to 9.9% in 3/89

Source: Bureau of Economic Analysis; Federal Reserve. Note: Percent changes are cumulative total.

Effects on the Financial Sector

Because efficient financial intermediation is vital to a healthy economy, if a housing downturn caused widespread harm to the financial sector, the overall economy could suffer.

A change in the value of a house has no direct effect on the value of a loan. But falling prices would be harmful to the financial system if homeowners responded by defaulting on existing loans [6]. While this strategy could be profitable in theory when the value of a mortgage exceeds the value of the home, in reality it seems unlikely given that houses are not solely investments to most homeowners and that people wish to maintain a good credit history. For the value of the mortgage to exceed the value of the house, even after prices have fallen, the loan would have to have a high loan-to-value ratio (a loan made fairly recently and probably to a first-time homeowner). It should be noted, however, that loan-to-value ratios have risen significantly in the past few years because homes are being purchased with smaller downpayments and because existing homeowners have borrowed against their equity.

To date, overall default rates have risen but remain low [7]. Default rates on subprime loans, loans made to borrowers with weak credit profiles, have risen more rapidly, however. Default rates on all adjustable rate mortgages (prime and subprime) have risen as well, and the problem may worsen in the near future as a significant share of existing mortgages are forecast to adjust to higher interest rates. To the extent that falling prices lead to rising defaults, it seems likely that it will be caused by the combination of falling prices and mortgage payments that borrowers cannot afford, either because of adjustable mortgages resetting to higher payments or because borrowers took on mortgages they could not really afford in the first place [8].

Mortgages that have lost value but are still current are unlikely to threaten a bank's overall health, but could lead the bank to curtail new lending through a balance sheet effect. When the value of a bank's assets declines, then its capital will also decline if its liabilities remain constant. The bank may then wish to replenish its capital by taking on fewer new loans. If banks make fewer loans, then all bank- financed projects could decline, including business capital investment.

Traditionally, bank regulation has been justified on the grounds that if losses on mortgages (or other loans) became widespread enough, the solvency of large segments of the banking sector could be at risk, and efficient financial intermediation could break down. Depository institutions have been required to hold adequate capital, adhere to prudent lending standards, and so on, to avoid this outcome.

Today, some mortgages are held by depository institutions and some are securitized and sold on the secondary market as mortgage backed securities (MBS). One rationale for the development of a secondary market was to move non-diversified risk off of bank balance sheets and disperse it throughout financial markets. So far, the increase in default rates has not resulted in any widespread problems for depository institutions, and the intermediation channel has continued to function smoothly. There is a fear, however, that as the mortgages underlying the MBS default, they will be brought back onto the bank's balance sheets, either through guarantees made to MBS investors or structured investment vehicles (SIVs.) [9].

Ironically, the housing downturn has instead led to widespread financial turmoil in secondary markets. The repricing of MBS to reflect the housing downturn has been untidy, leading to financial distress for many non-bank mortgage lenders that rely on securitization and for MBS investors. In August 2007, problems with MBS spilled over into other financial markets, leading to a widespread "liquidity crunch," in which financial intermediation ceased to function smoothly [10]. At this point, it is too soon to tell how quickly financial markets will recover from the liquidity crunch, and if the crunch will have lasting effects on economic activity.

Effects on Consumption

Many analysts have speculated that the housing boom had a positive "wealth effect" on personal consumption, which will become negative during a housing crash. Viewing housing as an asset from a life-cycle saving perspective, an increase in the value of that asset would increase an individual's potential lifetime consumption, assuming the asset would be liquidated at some point. The life-cycle theory suggests that the individual would wish to spread the consumption derived from the future income from the sale of the asset evenly over his lifetime beginning immediately. Since the theory predicts that consumption derived from the increased wealth would be spread over a lifetime, the increase in consumption in any given year would be very small. Evidence that the effect of a change in housing wealth is greater than a change in stock market wealth is mixed. One study estimated that households increase consumption by 0.08% for every 1% increase in housing wealth, which was about three times larger than the authors' estimate of a stock market wealth effect [11]. Another study estimated that households increased consumption by 0.03 %-0.09% for every 1% increase in housing wealth, compared with a 0%-0.07% increase in consumption for a 1% increase in stock market wealth [12]. Still, if housing wealth fell sharply, even small wealth effects can add up to large effects on the macroeconomy [13].

While this analysis has much to recommend it, there are some offsetting factors that could diminish the importance of a wealth effect on the overall economy. First, the proponents of the wealth effect tend to focus on the gains to the sellers, but the housing market is made up of both buyers and sellers. When prices increase, sellers are wealthier and can increase their lifetime consumption. But this is exactly offset by buyers, whose non-housing wealth falls when house prices go up (e.g., they will now have to borrow more to purchase the house and devote more of their income to repaying their mortgage). Thus, a change in housing prices causes an income transfer from buyers to sellers, which reduces the lifetime consumption of buyers by as much as the lifetime consumption of sellers is raised [14].

Second, there is another, more direct, channel through which a rise in housing wealth influences consumption: by reducing disposable or after-tax income. Most counties or municipalities levy a property tax as a percentage of the house's value, so that payment rises when a house's assessed value rises. This factor partially offsets any positive wealth effect.

Third, the life-cycle model makes several specific assumptions in determining whether or not consumption would be affected. The appreciation must be unexpected, since an expected appreciation would already have been incorporated into the individual's saving and consumption plans. The asset cannot be held until death. To finance higher lifetime consumption, it must at some point be liquidated, which is a problematic assumption with owner-occupied housing since the homeowner still needs to live somewhere after the asset is liquidated. To increase consumption upon the liquidation of a primary residence, the owner must move to a lower cost region or residence. (This is not the case for houses that are rented or secondary residences.) The riskiness surrounding the appreciation would also be an important determinant of how much consumption would increase when housing wealth increased. Some economists have argued that the wealth effect from housing is greater than the wealth effect from the stock market because gains in housing prices are less likely to be suddenly reversed. (The current state of housing markets might suggest otherwise.) In markets that had rapid appreciation, home owners may have felt hesitant to spend that wealth because of their uncertainty about whether or not the appreciation represented a bubble that would soon burst. If prices did subsequently fall but remained above pre-boom levels, this hesitancy may prevent consumption from falling significantly.

Consumption has remained strong to date. This is not surprising since the wealth effect would reduce consumption only if house prices fell. If prices instead stagnated, as they have so far, then consumption would not fall since household wealth would remain unchanged. CBO estimates that if house prices fell by 10% and consumption fell 2 cents per $1 in lost wealth, GDP growth would be reduced by 0.4 percentage points, while a wealth effect of 7 cents per $1 would reduce it by 1.4 percentage points [15]. If their assumptions accurately approximate reality, the wealth effect on consumption alone would not be enough to push the economy into recession.

The Household Debt Channel

The objections to the wealth effect raised in the previous section apply mainly to homeowners with unlimited access to credit. When homeowners are instead "liquidity constrained," a rise in house prices increases net housing equity and the potential to borrow. As access to credit increases, the ability to consume more increases, so a stronger wealth effect would be expected. This scenario would be consistent with rational households (who wish to smooth lifetime consumption) or households that borrow unsustainably. Of course, the number of homeowners who are liquidity constrained is arguably limited, given that homeowners tend to have above average credit histories and unsecured debt (e.g., credit cards) is prevalent in the U.S. economy.

While house prices were rising, homeowners increased their indebtedness rapidly, both because households financed bigger home purchases with smaller down payments and because they responded to rising prices by withdrawing equity from their homes through home equity loans (second mortgages) and refinancing. From 2002 to 2006, mortgage debt increased from $6.4 trillion to $10.4 trillion and home equity loans more than doubled to $1.1 trillion [16].

During the housing boom, some analysts argued that "mortgage equity withdrawal" (MEW) was fueling consumption spending. They argued that when many homeowners sold their homes or refinanced their mortgages, they were borrowing against some of their built up home equity to finance additional consumption spending [17]. This scenario can come about through an increase in the house's value (in which case, it can be seen as a manifestation of the "wealth effect") or a decrease in borrowing costs. A study by Alan Greenspan and James Kennedy estimated that four-fifths of the increase in mortgage debt since 1990 was the result of equity withdrawal [18].

If house prices were to fall or mortgage rates were to rise, this process could work in reverse. As long as households' borrowing is sustainable, a fall in house prices has no direct effect on consumption. But with higher indebtedness and falling house prices, there is the potential for the share of homeowners in distress to rise sharply in the near future. Compounding this risk is the impending reset of many adjustable rate mortgages to higher interest rates between now and 2009. If mortgage resets force homeowners to devote a larger share of their income to mortgage payments, their consumption spending could fall. Whereas struggling homeowners could withdraw equity to meet mortgage payments when prices were rising quickly, this option will no longer be available for many homeowners. Furthermore, lending standards have tightened and non-prime mortgage rates have risen since August 2007, making it less likely that mortgages will reset or be refinanced on favorable terms. Consumption purchases financed by borrowing could be curtailed as borrowing sources dry up, either because homeowners run out of home equity to tap or because default cuts off other sources of credit. This problem is likely to turn out to be more serious if the housing boom turns out to have been a bubble since it implies that more borrowers have gotten themselves into unsustainable situations.

How important is this factor quantitatively? In the second quarter of 2007, 0.65% of all mortgages entered foreclosure and the overall delinquency rate was 5.12%. Even assuming that all of these households reduced their consumption spending, overall consumption growth would still fall by a modest amount. While these rates are predicted to rise, even at the predicted rates, too few households would be affected to have a significant impact on overall consumption. Furthermore, the empirical evidence that mortgage equity withdrawal leads to higher consumption is mixed [19].

Overall Effect on the Economy

In the long run, economic theory states that housing cycles have no lasting effect on the economy because markets naturally adjust to reallocate resources. In the short run, a decline in economic activity via any of the four channels discussed above could lead to a slowdown in aggregate spending, but only if other sectors of the economy were unable to pick up the slack. Envision scenarios where other sectors would pick up the slack. For example, the current expansion has been characterized by a low national saving rate made up for by borrowing from abroad that comes to the United States in the form of a trade deficit. If falling house prices were to lead to lower consumption and higher saving, the effect on overall spending might be offset by a smaller trade deficit since foreign borrowing needs would diminish. Expansionary monetary or fiscal policy could also be used to offset any decline in spending, as will be discussed in a later section.

The strength of a housing crash's effect on the economy depends on the magnitude of the crash. While economic models predict that a fall in prices in the range that has been predicted would not single-handedly derail the economic expansion (see below for an example), some observers think it may be enough to tip an already tepid economy into recession. It could also make the expansion less capable of withstanding any additional unrelated shocks. Economic growth was below 3% for four straight quarters beginning in the second quarter of 2006, and, although it grew rapidly in second and third quarters of 2007, most forecasters had predicted it would remain tepid through the first half of 2008 even before the financial turmoil began in August 2007. Nonetheless, none of the 50 private sector forecasters surveyed by Blue Chip in October 2007 were predicting that the economy would enter a recession, although they have reduced their growth forecasts since August. Of course, the housing crash could turn out to be more severe than the forecasters are currently predicting, in which case their growth projections would be revised downward.

Macroeconomic Policy Response

A housing crash leads to lower economic growth through the channels described above only if all else remains equal. But the government need not remain idle and allow falling prices to feed through to lower economic growth. It can boost aggregate spending in the economy through expansionary fiscal or monetary policy. Expansionary fiscal policy refers to increases in the budget deficit; expansionary monetary policy refers to reductions in short-term interest rates [20]. Indeed, the Fed reduced interest rates by 0.5 percentage points on September 18, 2007, justifying the change on the grounds that "[w]ithout such policy action, members saw a risk that tightening credit conditions and an intensifying housing correction would lead to significant broader weakness in output and employment" [21] Ideally, expansionary policy and natural market adjustment can boost overall spending enough to offset any reduction in spending that resulted from the housing downturn. In reality, policymaking is hampered by enough lags and uncertainty that at times policy changes cannot prevent recessions. Policymakers err on the side of caution because if policy is too expansionary, inflation would rise to undesirable levels.

Based on simulations using the Federal Reserve's marcoeconomic model, Fed Governor Frederic Mishkin recently made the case that the Fed could largely offset the negative marcroeconomic effects of a housing crash even in what would presumably be the worst case scenario [22]. The first simulation assumes that house prices fall by 20% over two years — a much larger decline than has ever occurred in recent decades — and the Fed responds to the change in economic conditions in the same way it has in recent history. The simulation shows that by gradually reducing short-term interest rates by nearly 1 percentage point, the Fed can limit the reduction in GDP to 0.5% below the baseline at its trough. The effect on GDP comes from lower residential investment and consumption. Lower interest rates keep residential investment from declining significantly despite the fall in house prices — a surprising result given recent experience. The Fed model also makes conservative assumptions about the relationship between house prices and consumption, which, as noted above, is subject to a relatively wide band of uncertainty. Therefore, Governor Mishkin performs another simulation making alternative assumptions that the response of residential investment and household consumption to house prices is much stronger than assumed in the Fed's model. In this case, the 20% decline in prices causes GDP to fall 1.5% below the baseline at its trough — three times greater than predicted in the standard model, but still not enough to cause a recession.

Both of these results are based on an assumption that the Fed reacts as it has historically when it sees GDP and inflation fall below their baselines. But Mishkin argues that the Fed can further minimize the macroeconomic effect of a house price decline by reducing rates before lower house prices have fed through to lower GDP growth. In this case, GDP declines by only 0.25% under normal assumptions and 0.5% assuming house prices have stronger effects compared to the baseline. The Fed does not have to reduce interest rates further to achieve these results; it merely has to reduce them sooner. Essentially, the Fed can take advantage of the lag between the decline in house prices and its effect on the economy by putting expansionary policy in place in the meantime.

In reality, economic models cannot perfectly predict reality, and a decline in house prices could have additional negative ramifications for the economy that the simulation results do not capture. For example, it could reduce confidence or cause financial disruptions of the kind seen in August 2007. And the Fed, operating in an environment of uncertainty, may not be able to make the optimal policy choices that the simulation assumes. Nevertheless, the basic message that one can take away from these simulations is that, with the proper monetary policy response, even the effects of a much more severe housing crash than experienced to date would not be expected to cause a recession.

Empirical evidence suggests that the Fed's ability to counteract a housing downturn may be more limited than it used to be, however. One New York Fed study found that residential investment responds more slowly to a change in short-terms interest rates than in the past — it now takes two years for the change in interest rates to have its maximum effect [23]. According to Fed Chairman Ben Bernanke, the Fed estimates that residential investment's share of the economy's response to a change in short-term interest rates has fallen from 25% to 14%.24 Furthermore, the new channels through which mortgages are financed may not be as sensitive to monetary policy changes as the traditional banking channel. While this evidence may be bad news for the housing sector, it does not necessarily imply that monetary policy has become less effective overall, however.

As Governor Mishkin suggested, the sooner the Fed acts to offset a housing crash, the more limited the crash's effect on the economy would be. This has led some critics to argue that the Fed should go even further, and raise interest rates to try and deflate a housing bubble while it is forming. According to this logic, if a bubble is never allowed to form, then it cannot cause economic damage by bursting. Chairman Bernanke has pointed out two main drawbacks to this proposal.

If we could accurately and painlessly rid asset markets of bubbles, of course we would want to do so. But as a practical matter, this is easier said than done, particularly if we intend to use monetary policy as the instrument, for two main reasons. First, the Fed cannot reliably identify bubbles in asset prices. Second, even if it could identify bubbles, monetary policy is far too blunt a tool for effective use against them [25].

In other words, aggressively raising interest rates to counteract a bubble risks instigating the very recession that critics presumably wish to avoid [26].

Another critique of the Fed's current response to bubbles would be that although eliminating bubbles should not be a policy goal in and of itself, the Fed should have recognized that the housing bubble — like the stock market bubble before it — was a symptom of an overheating economy. By keeping interest rates too low, critics argue the Fed caused the economy to overheat and inflation to rise. As a result, the Fed has made a recession less avoidable and limited its room to maneuver to prevent it, because there is now the risk that rate cuts would increase inflation even further.

Previous Housing Crashes

In determining the likelihood of future house price declines, it useful to look at past declines. Since the house price index was first recorded in the 1970s, housing prices have never fallen in nominal terms on a national basis for more than one quarter, and when they fell, the decrease was more than reversed in the next quarter. However, house prices did fall in real (inflation-adjusted) terms nationwide in the early 1980s. From the second quarter of 1980 to the fourth quarter of 1983, house prices rose 15.6%, whereas overall inflation, as measured by the GDP deflator, rose by 26.6%. This trend seems easily explained by the change in economic fundamentals during that period: the economy in 1980-1982 featured historically high real interest rates and the worst economic recession in the post-war period. During this period, nominal mortgage rates peaked above 18% and the unemployment rate reached double digits. Although there have not been large nominal declines in housing prices historically, the housing market has been highly cyclical, with little appreciation in the early 1980s and early 1990s, and significant appreciation in the late 1980s and 1990s.

There have been historical examples of sharp nominal drops in local housing markets, however. A recent Federal Reserve study identified 17 states that experienced significant declines in housing prices in the 1980s or 1990s. All 17 episodes were linked to four specific economic shocks, which would point to some role for fundamentals — the farm and rust belt decline of the early 1980s, the drop in energy prices in the mid-1980s (which negatively affected energy-producing states), the downturn in New England in the late 1980s to early 1990s, and the downturn in California and Hawaii in the early 1990s (which the author links to the reduction in defense spending and Japanese financial crisis). Interestingly, most of the states affected by the first two shocks did not experience a preceding housing boom, ruling out a bubble. On balance, these examples seem to illustrate that recessions can cause house price declines, but do not speak to whether causation can run in the opposite direction. Further, the author identified several other housing booms in the 1980s and early 1990s that never resulted in housing declines, underlining the point that not all booms are followed by busts [27]. Another recent study identified historical housing booms and busts, and found that only nine housing booms (17% of the total) were followed by busts [28].

Figures 4, 5, and 6 focus on three cases, California, Texas, and New England, where a sharp prolonged increase in house prices was followed by a significant and prolonged nominal decline in house prices. In California, after rising about 75% in four years, nominal prices fell by 13.3% from the fourth quarter of 1990 to the first quarter of 1995. In Texas, after rising about 25% in five years (with most of the increase in the first two years), nominal prices fell by 14.4% from the first quarter of 1986 to the fourth quarter of 1988. In New England, after rising about 170% in six years, nominal prices fell by 12.9% from the first quarter of 1990 to the first quarter of 1995. In all three of the cases, although the trough of housing prices took several years to be reached, most of the decline occurred in a relatively short time.

In Texas, prices were 12.8% down from their peak by the fourth quarter of 1987; in New England, prices were down 10.6% by the third quarter of 1991. The pattern was a little different in California, where most of the decline occurred toward the end of the housing bust, rather than the beginning: prices fell 12.3% from the second quarter of 1992 to the first quarter of 1995.

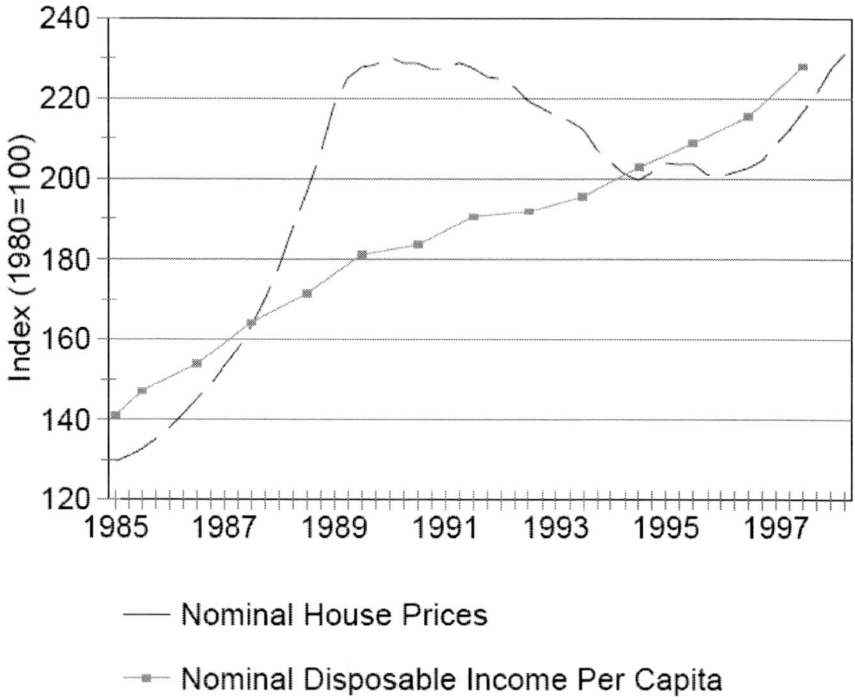

Source: Office of Federal Housing Enterprise Oversight, Bureau of Economic Analysis.

Figure 4. California Housing Bust.

All three areas took several years after the bust had ended to reach their previous peak, as seen in the figures. A hopeful sign for today is that, in each case, the crash did not reverse much of the prior appreciation.

It would be difficult to explain these price increases and subsequent declines — which are quite large in real terms — by macroeconomic factors alone. In each of these cases, while there were periods of rising (and falling) interest rates within each downswing, the episode as a whole could not be characterized as a period of rising interest rates. However, in each case, the local economy was experiencing a recession, although in each case the housing bust exceeded the length of the recession. In Texas, the state economy shrank 0.5% in 1987; in California, the economy shrank 1.9% from 1992 to 1993; and in New England, the economy shrank 4.6% from 1990 to 1991.

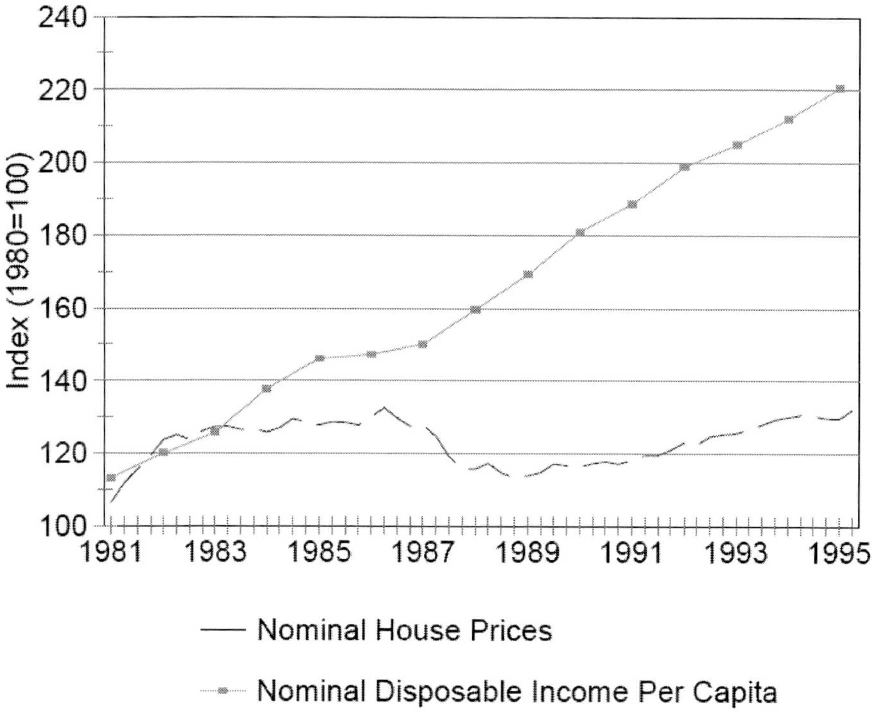

Figure 5. Texas Housing Crash.

In California and New England, a simple comparison of house prices and per capita disposable income suggests the pattern of house prices in the 1980s fits a bubble. During the boom, house price increases exceeded income gains. When house prices crashed, they were brought back into line with nominal income (which helps explain why house prices did not decline as much as they had previously risen). The Texas experience looks least like a classic bubble. There, the pattern is different: house prices never exceeded income during the boom, which was considerably smaller than the California and New England booms, and never caught up to income gains after the housing crash.

Parallels between past housing crashes and the current episodes are limited by changes to the housing market. These differences include the growing importance of mortgage securtiziation, the growth in subprime lending, the increase in the homeownership rate, and easier access to borrowing against home equity.

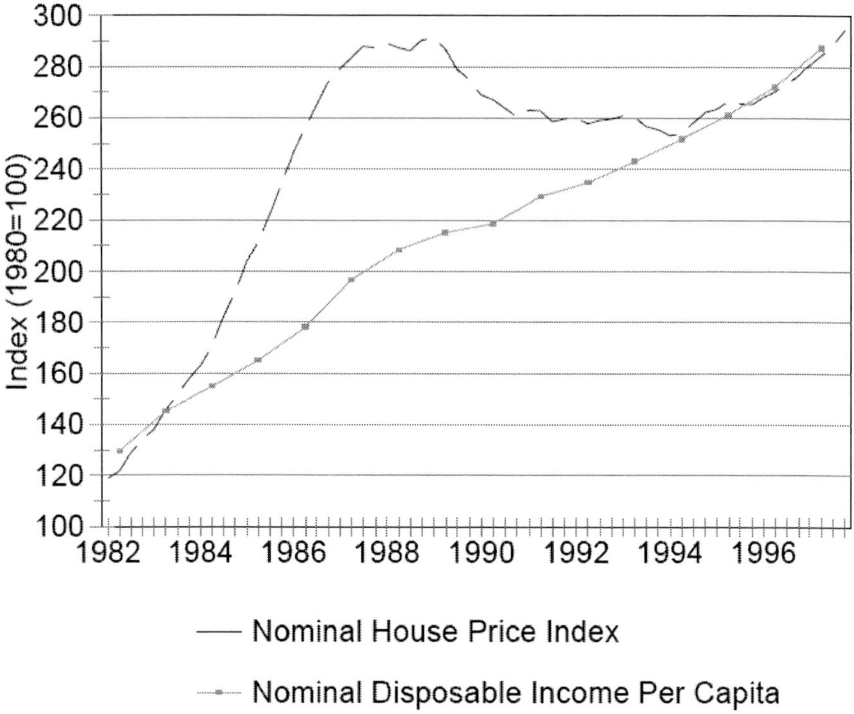

Source: Office of Federal Housing Enterprise Oversight, Bureau of Economic Analysis.

Figure 6. New England Housing Bust.

CONCLUSION

If a housing crash is defined as a significant decline in house prices, then the United States has not yet experienced a crash, although it cannot be ruled out in the future given the continuing fall in housing sales. Were house prices to fall gradually or stagnate, the economy is likely to be able to adjust without significant disruption. Were prices to drop sharply, the risk to the economy is much greater. If the boom was caused by a bubble, it implies that the housing downturn will probably get worse, and a sharp drop in prices is much more likely. Although changes in economic fundamentals, particularly lower mortgage rates, played an important role in the early years of the housing boom, it is difficult to identify non-bubble explanations for their unprecedented rise in the latter years.

If a housing crash is defined as a sharp decline in residential investment, then a crash has already occurred. Over the past five quarters, the rate of residential investment has declined by double digits and reduced overall GDP growth by an average of 1.0 percentage points, all else equal. While this drag on growth may persist in coming quarters, it is unlikely to get much larger. This suggests that the drag from the slowdown in house building could not cause a recession by itself.

Many economists have also predicted that a fall in prices would have a negative wealth effect on consumption. If so, and some doubts have been cast on this theory, the effect has not been strong enough to perceptibly reduce consumption yet. This is not surprising since the wealth effect predicts that stagnating (as opposed to falling) house prices, as seen so far, would not reduce consumption.

Another channel through which falling prices, combined with mortgage resets, could affect consumption would be if it led to a spike in mortgage default rates. While subprime default rates have risen sharply, the number of homeowners involved is too small to have much of a macro effect. But since the number of resets has not yet peaked and lending standards are tightening, the default rate could get worse.

Thus far, a more serious effect of the housing downturn has been the spillover of turmoil in financial markets, culminating in the August liquidity crunch. Widespread liquidity problems have the potential to interfere with the smooth functioning of financial intermediation that is necessary for robust economic growth. At this point, it is too soon to say whether the liquidity crunch has fed through to lower economic growth. Banks could also respond to falling house prices by curbing new lending since falling prices reduces the value of their assets.

To date, the sharp decline in residential investment has not disrupted the economic expansion, but since national prices have not yet fallen, it may be that the full effects of the downturn are yet to come. While it appears that a housing crash could not singlehandedly derail the expansion, it is possible that it could tip an already tepid economy into recession. Economic growth was below 3% for four straight quarters beginning in 2006:2, and, although it grew rapidly in second quarter of 2006, and, although it grew rapidly in second and third quarters of 2007, most forecasters had predicted it would be modest through the first half of 2008 even before the financial turmoil began in August 2007. Nonetheless, none of the 50 private sector forecasters surveyed by Blue Chip in October 2007 were predicting that the economy would enter a recession.

Were the housing market to crash, policymakers need not stand by and allow it to act as a drag on the overall economy. Indeed, the Federal Reserve has already reacted to the liquidity crunch by reducing short-term interest rates. Simulations by Fed Governor Frederic Mishkin suggest that the economic fallout from even a severe drop in housing prices could be modest if the Fed responds optimally.

On the other hand, some economists would argue that the Fed has already committed a policy error by not preventing what they characterize as a housing bubble from forming in the first place. While using monetary policy to target asset prices is likely to be problematic given the difficulty of identifying bubbles, one could argue that the current housing cycle of boom and bust has led to a less stable economy. If a housing crash were to lead to a recession, it would strengthen the argument that the Fed should take a less passive approach to asset bubbles in order to fulfill its mandate to maintain economic stability.

REFERENCES

[1] See CRS Report RL33666, Asset Bubbles: Economic Effects and Policy Options for the Federal Reserve, by Marc Labonte.

[2] This strategy may have been myopic, since an ARM improves affordability only until interest rates rise, and short-term interest rates were unusually low until 2004. If the decision was driven by myopia, it could be taken as more evidence of a bubble.

[3] See CRS Report RL33775, *Alternative Mortgages*, by Edward Murphy.

[4] "*The Global Housing Boom*," The Economist, June 18, 2005, p. 66.

[5] This figure measures the drag on GDP due to falling residential investment in an accounting sense. It does not represent the difference between overall GDP and the counterfactual case where residential investment does not fall, since it does not account for multiplier effects that could make the overall impact bigger, nor potential offsetting effects in other sectors that could make the impact smaller.

[6] Lower housing sales would require financial institutions to shift some of their activity from mortgage lending to other types of lending or investments. While this would not necessarily affect the overall profitability of the financial sector, some institutions might find the shift in lending difficult, particularly if they are small and heavily reliant on mortgage lending.

[7] Mortgage Bankers Association, "*Delinquencies Increase in Latest MBA Delinquency Survey*," press release, September 6, 2007.

[8] For information on mortgage resets, see CRS Report RL33775, Alternative Mortgages, by Edward Murphy.

[9] SIVs are off-balance sheet entities established (but not owned) by commercial banks. An SIV finances the purchase of long-term MBS by selling short-term notes and commercial paper. The spread between the long- and short-term rates is profit. For the concept to work, the SIV must be able to borrow cheaply — a triple-A rating is a basic requirement. To secure that rating, the SIV generally agrees to maintain certain levels of collateral and the sponsoring banks often commit themselves to providing lines of credit if the SIV becomes unable to raise funds in the market.

[10] See CRS Report RL34 182, Financial Crisis? The Liquidity Crunch of August 2007, by Darryl Getter, Mark Jickling, Marc Labonte, and Edward Murphy.

[11] John Benjamin, Peter Chinloy, and G. Donald Jud, "Real Estate Wealth Versus Financial Wealth in Consumption," *Journal of Real Estate Finance and Economics,* vol. 29, no. 3, 2004. The results are statistically significant at the 1% level.

[12] Karl Case, John Quigley, and Robert Shiller, Comparing Wealth Effects: The Stock Market Versus the Housing Market, National Bureau of Economic Research, Working Paper 8606, November 2001. The wealth effect for housing is statistically significant at the 1% level; the wealth effect for equities is statistically insignificant in some regressions.

[13] In the long run, there can be no net wealth effect from housing because consumption is determined by the economy's productive capacity, and a change in the price of an existing asset does not alter the economy's productive capacity. Thus, the wealth effect should be thought of as a short-term factor that affects the business cycle but has no lasting effect on long-term growth.

[14] A wealth transfer has no net change in consumption if buyers and sellers have the same marginal propensity to consume. The life-cycle model predicts that sellers would have a higher marginal propensity than buyers if they were much older, but empirical evidence casts doubt on this prediction since the elderly have higher saving rates and home ownership rates than the young.

[15] Congressional Budget Office, Housing Wealth and Consumer Spending, Background Paper no. 2834, January 2007.

[16] Federal Reserve, *Flow of Funds*, September 2007, Table L.218.

[17] Mortgage equity withdrawal does not lead to a one-to-one increase in consumption. For example, some of the equity withdrawn may be used to pay off other debt and some may finance consumption that would have occurred in any case.

[18] Alan Greenspan and James Kennedy, "Sources and Uses of Equity Extracted from Homes," *Federal Reserve, Finance and Economics Discussion Series* 2007-20, 2007.

[19] Greenspan and Kennedy, Op Cit, estimate that MEW was used to finance 1.75% of consumption spending from 2001 to 2005, but do not attempt to estimate how much of that spending would have occurred anyway. See also Macroeconomic Advisers, "Fear Not MEW," Macro Focus, vol. 1, no. 2, October 2006. Macroeconomic Advisers did not find any evidence that MEW Granger causes consumption, and in regressions results the variable was not statistically significant and had the wrong sign. See also Vladimir Kluyev and Paul Mills, "Is Housing Wealth an 'ATM'?", International Monetary Fund, working paper 06/162, July 2006. Kluyev and Mills found MEW to have a small (with the right sign) but statistically insignificant effect. Goldman Sachs, on the other hand, found a larger and statistically significant effect. See Jan Hatzius, "Housing Holds the Key to Fed Policy," *Goldman Sachs Economics Paper* no. 137, February 2006.

[20] For an in-depth discussion of fiscal and monetary policy, see CRS Report RL34072, Economic Growth and the Business Cycle, by Marc Labonte.

[21] Federal Reserve Board, "*Minutes of the Federal Open Market Committee*," September 18, 2007.

[22] Frederic Mishkin, "Housing and the Monetary Transmission Mechanism," working paper presented at the Federal Reserve Bank of Kansas City symposium, August 2007.

[23] Jonathan McCarthy and Richard Peach, "Monetary Policy Transmission to Residential Investment," Federal Reserve Bank of New York, *Economic Policy Review*, May 2002, p. 139.

[24] Chairman Ben Bernanke, "Housing, Housing Finance, and Monetary Policy," speech at the Federal Reserve Bank of Kansas City symposium, August 31, 2007.

[25] Ben Bernanke, "Asset Price 'Bubbles' and Monetary Policy," *Speech before the National Association of Business Economics,* New York, NY, October 15, 2002.

[26] For an in-depth discussion, see CRS Report RL3 3666, Asset Bubbles: Economic Effects and Policy Options for the Federal Reserve, by Marc Labonte.

[27] David Wheelcock, "What Happens to Banks When House Prices Fall?," Federal Reserve Bank of St. Louis, *Review,* vol. 86, no. 5, September 2006, p. 413.

[28] Federal Deposit Insurance Corporation, "U.S. Home Prices: Does Bust Always Follow Boom," FYI, May 2005. The study identifies booms as increases in real prices of at least 30% over three years and busts as declines in nominal prices of at least 15% in five years.

INDEX

9

A

B

C

D

G

H

I

J

L

M

R

S

T

U

V